# Who is the REAL Barack Obama?

## For the rising generation; by the rising generation

BY

STEVE BIERFELDT, FRANCISCO GONZALEZ, AND
BRENDAN STEINHAUSER

authorHOUSE®

*AuthorHouse™*
*1663 Liberty Drive, Suite 200*
*Bloomington, IN 47403*
*www.authorhouse.com*
*Phone: 1-800-839-8640*

*First published by AuthorHouse  8/11/2008*

*ISBN: 978-1-4389-0605-8 (sc)*

*Library of Congress Control Number: 2008907297*

*Printed in the United States of America*
*Bloomington, Indiana*

*This book is printed on acid-free paper.*

# CONTENTS

# INTRODUCTION

## THE *REAL* BARACK OBAMA

"Facts are stubborn things; and whatever may be our
wishes, our inclinations, or the dictates of our passion, they
cannot alter the state of facts and evidence."

- John Adams

The candidacy of Barack Obama has energized millions of Americans
who have turned out in record numbers to participate in the 2008
presidential primaries. Much of his candidacy's success has been built
upon the support he has among the youth and other new voters. So far,
Obama has won 18-29 year olds in every state, garnering 67% of their
votes in South Carolina, 59% in Nevada, 51% in New Hampshire
and 57% in Iowa. Granted, these numbers solely reflect the Democrat
primary. But, more young people (ages 18-29) are registered as Democrats
(43%) and independents (26%) than as Republicans (31%).[1]

Most of these young people often comment that Obama's flowery
speeches "inspire" them.[2] He has convinced them that he is the candidate
of "change." The only books published about Obama, however, have
been built on *his* narrative. Due to the lack of media scrutiny (and
the almost "giddiness" that much of the mainstream media has for
Obama), there is relatively little information available that questions or
challenges his candidacy in any serious way. As the recent controversies
surrounding his church, his pastor, and his other dubious associations

1

have demonstrated, when questions are raised, Obama has trouble answering them.[3]

Our book, written by three young voters, seeks to further expose Obama's background, his inexperience, his far left political agenda, and demonstrate that not all the youth are behind him. We also aim to challenge our peers (and others) to question their attraction to the Obama candidacy and his big government proposals. We believe that these proposals and Obama's far left beliefs that the government can solve our problems do not represent change, but simply the status quo. Real change would put power back in the people's hands, not more power concentrated in Washington. This, in fact, is the biggest problem in our political system and Obama doesn't want to "change" this crisis, he only wants to exacerbate it.

Why, then, have so many come to believe that Obama is an agent of "change you can believe in?" Mostly, we suppose, it is because the Obama campaign keeps using the word "change" and the media keeps following along. It is hard to find one interview, press conference, or rally where the Obama campaign has not strategically placed a sign (or a series of signs) that simply utilizes the word "change." If you keep saying something over and over again, people tend to believe it. Much to his campaign's credit (and the media's ability to repeat the mantra), "change" has thus become automatically associated with Obama. In a year when the poll numbers for both the incumbent Republican President and the Democrat Congress are as low as they can go, Americans certainly want "change." Obama's consistent use of the word "change" to describe his candidacy has been forcefully etched in voters' minds.

Obama's two books, *Dreams From My Father* and *The Audacity of Hope* are largely responsible for constructing the narrative about Obama that the mainstream media and the youth have followed at will. Both of these books have spent weeks on the *New York Times* best seller lists. Many books have been successfully published to challenge Hillary Clinton, who was supposed to be the "inevitable" Democrat nominee. But the media, the publishing industry, and the American people, have all been stunned by the apparent success of Obama. This has left a large hole in the publishing industry for books challenging the Obama campaign's crafted narrative. We hope this book will begin to fill part of that vacancy.

The reasons stated above are what drove us to write this book. We believe this book will arm voters with substantive research that they can use to learn more about where Obama stands on the important economic, national security, and social issues, and expose his background, character, and far left ideology. It is up to you, the reader, to digest this information, perhaps do some further research yourself, and then spread the factual evidence of what Obama really stands for.

We, the authors of this book, have had frequent contact with youth on college campuses. From this experience, we came to quickly realize that Obama is the candidate of choice among most college students today. Polls indicate this, but so do the emotions inside and outside the classroom. However, we have also experienced an undercurrent on college campuses, comparable to the "silent majority" that voted for Richard Nixon in 1968 and 1972. We do not believe the anti-Obama movement on college campuses represents any kind of majority, but we do believe there are more young people, like us, that are troubled about the possibility of an Obama presidency. Most of them are just too nervous to speak out against Obama, due to repercussions on campus by their professors and their peers.

College campuses today are the epitome of what it's like to be in the "Obamamania" circles. So, even if you're not on a college campus, but find yourself within these kinds of circles, you'll immediately realize what we're talking about. If you find yourself in one of these far left bubbles, and you're not voting for Obama, they will tell you that you must either be racist or you don't want to be a part of history (because if you haven't noticed, Obama would be the first black president). Never mind his ideology and his public policy positions: if you're a college student and you don't vote for Obama that would be comparable to not being a part of the civil rights movement in the 1960s.

When asked what Obama stands for, most who lend him credence can give no answer. Often, they simply say, "he's for change, aren't you for change?" When he flip-flops on positions, they go right along with him. Change is contagious, we suppose, even changing one's positions on important public policy issues.

Some follow Obama's mantra that he is not like other politicians and can "transcend" the usual conservative-liberal dichotomies. But a closer examination of his record and his votes shows that he is as far to the left as a politician can get. In fact, according to the *National Journal's* 2007 vote ratings of politicians, Obama was rated the most liberal U.S. Senator.[4] This is the same U.S. Senate that includes Senators Hillary Rodham Clinton, Barbara Boxer, Joe Biden, John Kerry, and Dianne Feinstein. Yes, he's further to the left than a San Francisco liberal.

In fact, that makes his comments at a fundraiser in San Francisco on April 6, 2008 all the more revealing. In trying to describe voters in the rural parts of Ohio and Pennsylvania, and why he wasn't doing well winning them over, here's what Obama told his liberal San Francisco audience:

> Here's how it is: in a lot of these communities in big
> industrial states like Ohio and Pennsylvania, people
> have been beaten down so long. They feel so betrayed by
> government that when they hear a pitch that is premised
> on not being cynical about government, then a part of
> them just doesn't buy it. And when it's delivered by — it's
> true that when it's delivered by a 46-year-old black man
> named Barack Obama, then that adds another layer of
> skepticism…
>
> … But the truth is, is that, our challenge is to get people
> persuaded that we can make progress when there's not
> evidence of that in their daily lives. You go into some of
> these small towns in Pennsylvania, and like a lot of small
> towns in the Midwest, the jobs have been gone now for 25
> years and nothing's replaced them. And they fell through
> the Clinton administration, and the Bush administration,

and each successive administration has said that somehow these communities are gonna regenerate and they have not. And it's not surprising then they get bitter, they cling to guns or religion or antipathy to people who aren't like them or anti-immigrant sentiment or anti-trade sentiment as a way to explain their frustrations.

Yes, ladies and gentleman: a man running for the American Presidency just described people in small towns as "bitter," which makes them "cling to guns or religion" and that when they get frustrated, they become xenophobic towards immigrants and foreign trade. (And never mind the comment that they are cynical about government: weren't our founders just as cynical?) With elitist sentiments such as these, as the American President, Obama will bring in his own antipathy towards Americans that he just doesn't understand: those people in small towns that "cling to guns or religion."

It is important to keep in mind that Obama made these statements while speaking at a fundraiser. His audience was a far left crowd in San Francisco. These comments were no mistake. He knew exactly the right buzz words to tell that audience in order for them to donate to his campaign and energize them to volunteer for him. He wanted them to feel that he was "one of them" and not one of "those" rural voters who believe in God and the second amendment of the U.S. Constitution.[5] With these comments, Obama did not "transcend" the partisan divide, but rather allied himself with the values of San Francisco liberals. So he was either being a typical politician by playing on *their* emotions out in San Francisco, or he is lying to all of us when he tells us he can transcend the partisan divide. These comments are only one of many examples we will bring you in this book to show you who Barack Obama really is.

This book is categorized in two different sections. In the first section, we detail Obama's policies on "the issues," which include foreign policy, economic policy, health care, immigration and culture, and social issues concerning the family and human life.

Brendan Steinhauser writes the chapters about Obama's foreign policy and economic policy. In a post-9/11 world, America has projected strength and has terrorist groups like Al-Qaeda on the run. We may not all agree on the best methods of fighting the enemy, but an Obama presidency will be disastrous and cripple our ability to win the war and face down tyrants and terrorists. Obama has already said that as President he would sit down with dictators in Iran, North Korea, Cuba, Venezuela, and others "without preconditions."

Of course we all want to further diplomacy and sometimes that includes talking to our enemies. But U.S. policy is always strongest when *we* decide how negotiations should go forward, not when we capitulate to our enemy's demands and meet with them "without preconditions." In his first four years as President, Ronald Reagan did not sit down with any leaders from the Soviet Union as so many of his predecessors did during the Cold War. Finally, after communist leaders kept dying on him, the Soviet Union produced a reformist who could deal with the United States: Mikhail Gorbachev. When the appropriate time came, Reagan agreed to a meeting – only to walk out on Gorbachev when the talks started breaking down. Sparing the rest of the details, a few years later, the Berlin Wall came down and the Soviet Union crumbled, "without firing a shot."

From explaining why the terrorist group Hamas is supporting Obama to detailing Obama's proposed massive social experiment to educate the Muslim world, Steinhauser details why Obama's foreign policy, while perhaps well-intentioned, will set America back in the war against radical Islamic terrorism. Obama won't reduce America's role in the world, but only increase it in other ways.

Next, Steinhauser will bring us a detailed look into Obama's economic policies, which will introduce massive new government spending and increased taxes. If we continue with the status quo, entitlement spending by the federal government will remain a huge and growing problem. Instead of bringing real "change" to the federal budget by reducing the demands on it, Obama wants to not only increase spending, but start new entitlement programs, such as government health insurance (which is detailed more fully in a chapter by Steve Bierfeldt) and foreign aid programs. President George W. Bush has spent more money abroad on foreign aid to places like Africa, Latin America, and Asia, than any other President in U.S. history. Obama wants to make President Bush's increased spending look like a footnote in history, as the U.S. taxpayer keeps footing the bill.

While he constantly speaks about how he will "transcend" partisan divides, Obama persistently engages in class warfare rhetoric and his policies continue the old left's socialist experiment of redistributing income. America was built on the idea of the individual work ethic. You produce it, you earn it, you own it, you keep it, you decide how you should share it. Obama wants government to play a bigger role in the owning, keeping, and sharing, thus reducing the individual liberties of all Americans.

In a time when all kinds of expenses are rising on the American consumer, Obama wants to increase their taxes. His energy policy will also insure that gas prices keep rising. In fact, he even said he supports rising gas prices, he just wishes they could rise more gradually. "I think that I would have preferred a gradual adjustment... to encourage the market to adapt to these circumstances, particularly U.S. automakers."[6] Steinhauser links Obama's energy policies to his "green" ideology. Environmental extremists make the same argument as Obama: they want energy prices to rise so that Americans stop using so much of it. And, through a "carbon cap," Obama wants to tax Americans so that higher energy costs will prevent Americans from continuing to live as they please and force them into conservation.

After we have tried to find ways that Obama's plans will "stimulate" the economy, Steve Bierfeldt will detail Obama's plans for yet another entitlement program: government health care. As CATO Institute fellow P.J. O'Rourke once said, "If you think health care is expensive now, wait until you see what it costs when it's free." With Obama's plan, we'll get the same health care system we have now (at best), with a government bureaucracy attached to it. If we don't yet have health care plans that pay for our medical expenses, the government will pay for it for us. How are they going to do that? More taxes, of course. And if you think illegal immigrants who don't pay taxes won't be able to get government-provided health care, think again.

In his second chapter, "Citizens of the Republic," Steve Bierfeldt details Obama's views on immigration and culture. Obama voted to provide free education (yes, in-state tuition and taxpayer-provided scholarships!) for illegal immigrants. By detailing Obama's votes and his quotes, Bierfeldt demonstrates how Obama continues to display a disdain for the rule of law and hard-working American taxpayers. It is no wonder why Obama had such a problem with working-class voters in the Democrat primaries in Ohio and Pennsylvania.

Francisco Gonzalez will detail where Obama stands on abortion, same-sex unions, and other issues that affect the most important unit of American life: the family. Among many of his radical stands on social issues, Obama's own voting record is deplorable on the simple act of protecting our children. He has voted against filtering pornography on elementary school computers and voted against legislation that would require that babies that survive abortions be cared for, instead of left to die. There is no room for nuance in these important issues that literally affect human lives and the livelihood of the family. Is this change we can believe in?

The second section of the book will be devoted to Obama's character and ideology. Gonzalez will give us a history of Obama's religious experience: from his Muslim heritage; to being raised by his mother, a secular atheist; to his discovery of Christianity at the controversial Trinity United Church of Christ, while he was a community activist in Chicago. As Gonzalez will explain, Obama's view of Christianity is tainted by the heresy of liberation theology, which is a blend of Christian and Marxist beliefs. Such beliefs have been condemned by orthodox Catholics such as Popes John Paul II and Benedict XVI and evangelical Christian leaders like James Dobson and Tony Perkins.

Gonzalez raises the importance of Obama's religious background – from his Muslim heritage to the liberation theology preached at Trinity United

Church of Christ – because Obama uses so much biblical language in his speeches and texts. He has stated how much his church and his pastor have influenced him. Since he has self-claimed that his heritage and his faith experience have made him who he is, we as voters are obligated to question how it will influence his ideology, his character, and his public policies.

In his third chapter, Gonzalez links Obama's tainted religious beliefs to his socialist policies. This particular chapter was chosen to follow the preceding one because it is intended to show how Obama's appeal to religious voters should make such voters wary – not only because Obama has been part of a fringe religious group for the past twenty years, but also because he and his church have conformed their religious beliefs to their preconceived political beliefs. The argument Gonzalez makes is plain and simple: Barack Obama's policies endorse the idea of big government solutions, social welfare, and the redistribution of income. For Senator Obama, his solution for our nation is to put the leftist policies that align with the liberation theology preached at Trinity United Church into practice. He has already done so as an Illinois state senator and during his short time as a U.S. Senator; there is no reason to doubt that he'll continue these far left policies from the White House.

The final chapter, "Misplaced Loyalty," by Bierfeldt, puts the nail in the coffin on why we cannot trust Barack Obama. Bierfeldt shows how Obama and his campaign staff have repeatedly contradicted themselves on the issue of Obama's "lost records" from his time as an Illinois State Senator. He does not have much experience to run on, one would think the few records he does have would be easy to find. Obama repeats over and over again about his desire to bring transparency to Washington D.C. and the office of the President. But, his actions don't speak as loud as his words.

***

Once we dug a littler further ourselves and examined the evidence, we saw that the picture Obama has painted of himself – a picture that most of the media follows like adoring fans – became distorted. It was no longer the same image. It is for this reason that we decided to spend our time and effort to do the research and present the facts about Obama as they are. As John Adams said, "Facts are stubborn things." We do not intend to make this book a long editorial. Rather, we have sought to make a case, based on the facts, that Obama is not who he wants you to think he is. Whether or not you agree with his policies, we think that after you examine the evidence, you will begin to peel away the fiction, fizzle out the hype, and unmask the *real* Barack Obama.

# ENDNOTES

[1]     Center for Information and Research on Civic Learning and Engagement, http://www.civicyouth.org/quick/youth_voting.htm

[2]     David Von Drehle, "The Year of the Youth Vote," *TIME*, http://www.time.com/time/politics/article/0,8599,1708570,00.html (31 January 2008).

[3]     Rick Pearson and John McCormick, "Barack Obama takes heat over NAFTA memo, Rezko: Clinton questions rival Democrat's credibility," *Chicago Tribune*, http://www.chicagotribune.com/news/chi-campaign_04mar04,0,5412950.story, (4 March 2008).

[4]     Brian Friel, Richard Cohen, and Kirk Victor, "Obama: Most Liberal Senator in 2007," *National Journal,* http://nj.nationaljournal.com/voteratings, (31 January 2008).

[5]     Jake Tapper, Jake "'Bitter' Pill Hard to Swallow in Pennsylvania Town," *ABC NEWS*, http://abcnews.go.com/WN/story?id=4652934, (14 April 2008); Mark Halperin,, "Transcript of Obama's Remarks at San Francisco Fundraiser Sunday," *TIME*, http://thepage.time.com/transcript-of-obamas-remarks-at-san-francisco-fundraiser-sunday, (7 April 2008).

[6]     Ed Morrissey, "Obama: I'd like higher gas prices, just not so quickly," *Hot Air*, http://hotair.com/archives/2008/06/11/obama-id-like-higher-gas-prices-just-not-so-quickly, (11 June 2008).

# PART ONE: THE ISSUES

# CHAPTER 1

## NOT READY ON DAY ONE:
## BARACK OBAMA'S FOREIGN POLICY

Once President George W. Bush leaves office in early 2009 a new president will enter the stage and inherit an uncertain and dangerous world. That president will face many foreign policy challenges, including the rise of China, Russia's resurgent nationalism, Islamic terrorism, Iran's pursuit nuclear weapons and humanitarian crises in Africa. The new president will also have the challenge to exit Iraq honorably while leaving behind a stable situation.

To examine Senator Barack Obama's foreign policy views, I have turned primarily to his article in *Foreign Affairs* in July 2007, where he laid out his vision for United States foreign policy. Obama has made many statements in the debates and interviews he has participated in, but I decided to rely mostly upon his own printed words, in context, to decipher his beliefs concerning the role of the United States in the world. Upon reading and thinking about his vision for American foreign policy, it is clear that Obama is not ready to face the challenges of the 21$^{st}$ century threats we face. His leftist worldview seems to prevent him from understanding the true nature of the threat of militant Islam, and his plans for defeating the enemy are weak and misdirected.

Senator Obama begins his article in *Foreign Affairs* by writing, "The American moment is not over, but it must be seized anew. We must bring the war to a responsible end and then renew our leadership—military, diplomatic, moral—to confront new threats and capitalize on new opportunities."[7] Obama acknowledges that the world is a dangerous place. He mentions the threat to America from "rogue states allied to terrorists" that convinced many in the Bush administration that Saddam Hussein could not be allowed to rule in a post 9-11 world. He cites the problem of "loose nukes" and an aggressive Iran.

Obama writes that dangerous al Qaeda elements remain in the Pakistan and Afghanistan hinterlands. He argues that we must refocus on these areas by increasing aid and diplomacy to prevent a resurgent Taliban. And he notes the rise of China, which could pose a serious threat to United States interests in the near future. Throughout the article Obama tries to portray himself as a centrist on foreign policy. Many of his recommendations for rebuilding the military, rebuilding our alliances with allies and applying tougher sanctions on Iran would be supported by most conservatives. But Obama's glaring omission in his foreign policy plan is a serious effort to defeat al Qaeda in Afghanistan, Pakistan, Iraq and elsewhere.

Obama spends very little time explaining how he will utilize the military, including special forces, to win on the battlefields where we are currently engaged. Instead, he briefly describes how he will "insist" that Pakistan do more to fight al Qaeda in its peripheral areas. He immediately turns to the volatile situation in Kashmir, and argues that if we solve that problem somehow Pakistan will be less likely to cooperate with the Taliban. Obama rightly points out the need to improve our human intelligence capabilities, but somehow forgets to tie this in with the fight underway against al Qaeda in Pakistan, Afghanistan and Iraq. What use is human intelligence if it is not deployed on the battlefields where it is most needed?

As for the rest of his "comprehensive" strategy to defeat the terrorists, Obama endorses nation-building on a grander scale than even the most fervent neoconservatives support. He plans to "strengthen weak states and help to rebuild failed ones." If the experiment in Iraq was, as Obama claims, a failure, then why would he support spending billions of dollars and deploying thousands of troops and civilians to sustain foreign societies?

The conflict in his rhetoric is striking. He believes the United States should "export opportunity—access to education and health care, trade and investment—and provide the kind of steady support for political reformers and civil society that enabled our victory in the Cold War." Is this not the kind of meddling, intrusive, imperialist impulse that led the United States into Iraq, or which has bred hatred and resentment in places like Egypt, Pakistan, Iran and the Palestinian territories over the years? Most leftists seem to think so. If the Islamists hate the United States now, wait until President Obama launches his campaign to properly educate the Muslim world on *our* terms. If we invest more money in that part of the world, won't the Islamists say that the United States seeks to destroy their way of life in the form of economic and cultural imperialism? If we support the democratic movements in the Muslim world, won't the Islamists have proof of our intentions to impose dreaded "democracy" not just with the gun but with our wealth and influence? How does any of this make us any safer?

Are these positions a reflection of cognitive dissonance or of Obama's doublespeak on foreign affairs? If the Bush legacy was an "arrogant" foreign policy that caused the world to resent United States power and influence, how will an Obama presidency be any better? Isn't Obama simply continuing the Bush legacy in a different form? Instead of imposing democracy with the military, President Obama would impose it through civilian bureaucracies. If those that argue that the Muslim world dislikes us because of our foreign policy are correct, won't Muslims continue to dislike us if we continue our interventionist, paternalistic and arrogant foreign policy?

Here, Obama may actually be at odds with his leftist friends who blame the U.S. for 9-11 and the resulting war against al Qaeda and its allies. This makes one wonder whether Obama really intends to "change" our grand strategy, or if he was just pandering to the left to get the Democrat nomination. Now that he has the nomination, Obama will likely try to move more to the center in his speeches and debates with Senator

McCain. This indicates that Obama is either a phony when it comes to foreign affairs, or is beginning to realize how McCain's *gravitas* on national security will force him to appear tougher and more realistic.

Let us turn, then, to the merits of Obama's plan for the Muslim and Arab world. If we take him at his word, Obama will solve the world's problems with an expensive and ambitious globalized effort never seen before. Not content to introduce a large dose of socialism on the domestic front, Obama's overarching plan to make the world safe from terrorists is a massive dose of socialism for the Muslim and Arab world. He writes, "Since extremely poor societies and weak states provide optimal breeding grounds for disease, terrorism and conflict, the United States has a direct national security interest in dramatically reducing global poverty." His remedy is a $2 billion Global Education Fund to reduce the "education deficit" in the world. Obama seems to be treating terrorism as the byproduct of disaffected youth that did not have the opportunity to go to college. But since Mohammed Atta, Dr. Ayman al Zawahiri, Ramzi Yousef and many other notorious Islamist terrorists were far from "uneducated," (they attended Western universities and come from families with high income backgrounds) Obama's rationale for spending billions of dollars on the education of foreign populations is misguided.

Unfortunately, this idea is to be expected from a leftist academic who actually wrote the following utopian statement about the goal of his global fund: "[The fund is meant] to ensure that every child everywhere is taught to build and not to destroy." Thomas Dewey or Jean Jacques Rousseau could not have said it better. If only we can reach all the hundreds of millions of children in the world with our message of "hope" they will not want to set off roadside bombs or shoot innocent civilians. Obama's fundamental belief in the power of the state to change human nature is frightening but predictable for someone on the far left of the political spectrum.

While Obama would launch a full-scale, massive social experiment for most of the Muslim world, he would retreat in the face of the enemy in Iraq. He writes that he would "begin a phased withdrawal of U.S.

forces, with the goal of removing all combat brigades from Iraq by March 31, 2008." It is clear that if he were president now, he would enact this policy to end the war in Iraq. But although Obama foresaw the problems of going into Iraq in the first place, he was wrong on the so-called "surge" policy that McCain pushed for – what has become the current winning strategy in Iraq.

While it was hugely unpopular at the time, McCain argued that Iraq needed more troops – not less – to reduce violence and rid Iraq of al Qaeda. Once the surge was in place and began to achieve its military and political goals, McCain's presidential campaign picked up support. But Obama has never had to answer for his opposition to the new counterinsurgency strategy that has made things measurably better in Iraq.

Even the editors of the *Washington Post* urged Obama to change his position on Iraq. In late May they pointed out that when Obama was pushing withdrawals from Iraq, the war was not going well. But they noted that as the surge has been working, Obama needed to come up with something to fit this new paradigm. The editors of the *Washington Post* wrote, "Now [Obama] needs a plan for success."[8] If Obama does not adjust to this new reality, then the American people can rightly question his judgment on foreign policy. Retaining his leftist ideology on Iraq in the face of a new reality on the ground will call into question his readiness to be Commander-in-Chief.

Obama wrote in *Foreign Affairs* that "we must launch a comprehensive regional and international diplomatic initiative to help broker an end to the civil war in Iraq, prevent its spread, and limit the suffering of the Iraqi people." On this point, he will find little opposition from conservatives. Iraqi politicians certainly need to hear from their neighbors and receive pressure from the international community to move forward on political reconciliation.

Obama follows this up by suggesting that the U.S. make it clear we seek no permanent bases in Iraq and that we leave only an "over-the-horizon military force in the region" to protect Americans, train Iraqi forces and root out al Qaeda. If the U.S. were to do this, and al Qaeda began to resurface in places where they have already been rooted out, would Obama support another military offensive, even on a limited scale? It seems so, which is a reasonable position. But given the fact that al Qaeda remnants remain in Iraq and U.S. forces are currently killing or capturing more of them every month, doesn't it make sense to allow the troops to finish the job before re-deploying?

Whatever Obama's position on Iraq, his credibility is questionable given that he has not traveled to Iraq in more than 900 days. While other Democrat politicians have traveled to Iraq and made their own assessment of the situation on the ground, Obama has not done so.[9] When General David Petreaus came to Washington multiple times to testify in front of the Senate about the situation in Iraq, Obama never requested a personal discussion. Still, Obama maintains his ideological views on Iraq, and seemed disinterested in talking one-on-one to the commander responsible for our efforts there.

Even though Obama claims that he would rather focus on the war against al Qaeda and its allies in Afghanistan, he has shown very little interest in that country, despite the fact that he is the chairman on the Senate subcommittee that overseas that operation. This seriously calls into question his supposed concern for our efforts in Afghanistan and Iraq, and should give the American people pause when they consider his experience and judgment for overseeing our military. His rhetoric says one thing, but his actions say another, which only reinforces the problem of authenticity that Obama has when it comes to his ideas for foreign policy.

Speaking of Obama's authenticity problem, one cannot fail to mention his conflicting views about the U.S. relationship with the state of Israel. Obama has gone from a supporter of the Palestinian cause to a supposedly staunch supporter of Israel as a Jewish state. During his time as an Illinois state senator Obama expressed support for the Palestinian cause. As Ali Abunimah noted on his website *Electronic Intifada*, Obama was his state senator and expressed a very pro-Palestinian position for years. In fact, Abunimah, a pro-Palestinian activist in Chicago, related a story about Obama's campaign to win a congressional seat in Illinois. Abunimah wrote that Obama told him, "Hey, I'm sorry I haven't said more about Palestine right now, but we are in a tough primary race. I'm hoping when things calm down I can be more up front."[10]

The admission of pure political pandering is quite striking. Abunimah says that Obama attended fundraisers and other events promoting the Palestinian cause throughout the years. Abunimah even posted a picture on his website of Obama and his wife Michelle at a pro-Palestinian event with Edward Said as the keynote speaker. The Obamas were at the table with Said, who was known for his militantly pro-Palestinian and anti-Western positions. Said once called the Bush administration an "American Taliban" and said that Yassir Arafat was too moderate.

Obama's early views on Israel and the Palestinians may come back to haunt him with voters who see the U.S. relationship with Israel to be an important part of our foreign policy. Even as late as March 2007, while on the campaign trail, Obama showed quite a bit of sympathy for the Palestinian people. "Nobody is suffering more than the Palestinians", he told a crowd in Iowa.[11] Apparently, Hamas, the terrorist group that controls the Gaza Strip was so impressed with Obama's views on the Middle East that the group endorsed him as their preferred candidate. Hamas' political advisor, Ahmed Yousef, told WABC radio station, "We like Mr. Obama and we hope he will win the election."

While pro-Palestinian activists and the current regime running Gaza are familiar with Obama's previous statements and positions, he has seemingly changed his views more recently. At a gathering of the American Israel Public Affairs Committee in June 2008, Obama called himself "a true friend of Israel" and said that Israel's security is "sacrosanct" and "non-negotiable."[12]

Obama has also struck a harsh chord when it comes to the threat posed by Iran, saying, "The danger from Iran is grave, it is real, and my goal will be to eliminate this threat." This is a far cry from the statement Obama had previously made on the campaign trail that "Iran doesn't pose a serious threat to us."[13]

To add to this doublespeak, in the AIPAC speech Obama labeled the Iranian Revolutionary Guard al Quds force "a terrorist organization." But when he had the opportunity to vote on whether or not the Senate should declare this to be the case, Obama did not show up for the vote. Then he told the press that if he had shown up to vote on the resolution, he would have voted against it.[14]

When reviewing Obama's changing and contradictory positions on Israel, the Palestinians and Iran, it is clear that he wants to have his cake and eat it too. No one can know for sure what his views are, but it is clear that his authenticity on these questions is seriously in doubt.

Obama's foreign policy worldview is shaped by the materialist view that where poverty, disease and ignorance simmer, violence boils to the surface. His willingness to sit down with communist or Islamist dictators like Raul Castro, Kim Jung Il or Mahmoud Ahmadinejad displays his naïve belief in the innate reasonableness of tyrannical leaders. As Sociologist-in-Chief, Obama would try to understand "why they hate us." He would try to ameliorate the supposed conditions that give rise to extremism and violence.

Obama's worldview is in line with the modern leftist view of the world: If only the United States would do more to set a good example, treat every world leader with respect and engage in a less militaristic or unilateral foreign policy, we could all enjoy world peace. Unfortunately, Obama's understanding of the causes of terrorism and dictatorship is incomplete, at best. Given human nature, there will always be evil in the world. While utilizing the full tool kit of statecraft, including traditional diplomacy, public diplomacy, economic sanctions and military force are good ideas, believing that you can always change people's behavior through policy is a mistake. The Muslim world has many good people that want nothing but peace and prosperity for their families. But it also contains an uncompromising, nihilistic Islamist movement that seeks the destruction of all those outside the Muslim faith, those called the *dhimma*. Until Obama comes up with a serious plan for defeating this dangerous movement of extremists, he is not ready to be our Commander-in-Chief.

The most fundamental difference between the left and the right on foreign policy is the question of why we are at war with Islamist terrorist groups around the world in the first place. Obama seems to agree with the leftist view that where poverty, ignorance and hopelessness prevail, terrorism is the natural result. He believes that the best way to fight terrorism is to fight the so-called "root causes" of terrorism. This means that a President Obama would spare no expense to pour billions of dollars into foreign aid and development projects in the Muslim and Arab world. Conservatives, on the other hand, view the battle as an ideological struggle with an unrelenting and evil enemy that seeks the destruction of all *infidels*. They view the war against Islamists as the next long-term battle, which some commentators have called World War IV. In this view, the struggle against al Qaeda and other Islamists will require decades of ideological warfare, covert operations, conventional military force and preventing "failed states."

While Obama is willing to use force in limited ways in Iraq, Afghanistan and even Pakistan, he wants to spend too much of our energy on a massive social engineering experiment in the Muslim and Arab world. If Islamist terrorists attacked U.S. targets and personnel because of the terrible conditions in which they live, why are we not under attack from poor people in places like Sub-Saharan Africa, India, or Latin America? Why is it that so many of the Islamist *mufsidoon* that attack us are well-educated and wealthy? Osama bin Laden, Mohammed Atta and many others were not hungry, poor or uneducated. Rather, they were driven by an extreme hatred of the West and all those outside the Muslim community.

Indeed, there is a ring of fire that surrounds the Muslim world from Morocco, to Sudan, to the Caucasus, to India and China, to the Philippines and to Indonesia. The one commonality that binds these murderous extremists is their perverted ideology, militant Islam. What is it that makes someone like John Walker Lindh or Adam Gadahn become so demented that they hate their own country and go to train with those that have killed their fellow citizens? It is not poverty, nor lack of a Harvard education. These two Americans joined the Islamist cause because they converted to Islam and took up the militant strain that encourages its adherents not to love life, but to love death.

Extremist ideologies – whether revolutionary communism, National Socialism or militant Islam – unite believers around a common revolutionary goal. Everything outside of that supreme goal is rejected, while everything and everyone can be sacrificed to its end. Militant Islam is simply the next evil ideology that threatens the West, and indeed, the rest of the world. The biggest victims of militant Islam are regular Muslims who happen to be in the way of the terrorists. Only a strong coalition of moderate Muslims, the West and the rest of the world can defeat such a nihilistic cult of death-worship.

It is this fundamental truth that Obama simply does not seem to understand. When judging a candidate's readiness to be Commander-in-Chief, understanding their overall worldview matters very much. If the candidate views Islamic terrorism as a threat to be dealt with by a New Deal for Muslims and Arabs, then that candidate does not take the threat seriously enough. That candidate fails to understand the true nature of the enemy, and should not be given the privilege and responsibility of leading The United States as its Commander-in-Chief. Obama has not only been deceptive about his own authentic foreign policy positions, but he has also shown a naïveté and lack of judgment in this area, and does not have the experience, nor the correct understanding of our enemies to keep our nation safe.

# Endnotes

7    Barack Obama, "Renewing American Leadership", *Foreign Affairs*, http://www.foreignaffairs.org/20070701faessay86401/barack-obama/renewing-american-leadership.html (July/August 2007).

8    Editorials, "The Iraqi Upturn", *Washington Post*, http://www.washingtonpost.com/wp-dyn/content/article/2008/05/31/AR2008053101927.html, (1 June 2008).

9    As of publication of this book in July 2008, Obama had not been to Iraq in more than 900 days. However, political pressure was beginning to build against Obama, as John McCain and other critics of Obama's policies suggested he needed to take a trip to Iraq and Afghanistan before the November 2008 election.

10    Ali Abuminah, "How Barack Obama learned to love Israel", *Electronic Intifada*, http://electronicintifada.net/v2/article6619.shtml, (4 March 2007).

11    Thomas Beaumont, "Obama urges more compassion in Middle East", *The Politico*, http://www.politico.com/news/stories/0307/3082.html, (13 March 2007).

12    Barack Obama speech at the American Israel Public Affairs Committee, June 4, 2008.

13    Barack Obama speech, Oregon, May 18, 2008; Ed Morrissey, "Iran not a 'serious threat'?" http://hotair.com/archives/2008/05/19/iran-not-a-serious-threat/, (19 May 2008).

14    Helene Cooper, "Clinton's Iran Vote: The Fallout," *New York Times*, http://www.nytimes.com/2007/10/14/weekinreview/14cooper.html, (14 October 2007).

# CHAPTER 2

## BREAKING THE BUDGET:
## ENTITLEMENT PROGRAMS AND TAXATION

Just as important as a nation's national security is its economic strength. For the United States to remain a world power and *the last best hope of mankind on earth* it must have a vibrant economy, a strong currency and a favorable climate for foreign investment. If Senator Obama is elected president, his plans to increase taxes and spending will cripple the economy and put us down the path toward financial disaster. At a time when there is growing uncertainty about the U.S. economy, the last thing this country needs is a policy of tax, redistribute and spend.

This chapter will examine Obama's statements and votes on economic issues, including taxes, spending, entitlements, trade and regulations. Upon reviewing Obama's economic views, it becomes clear that he plans to outdo previous explosions in the size and scope of government. While many parts of the world are becoming more economically free, Obama would restrict our economic freedom through a number of costly and burdensome programs and regulations. His election would make the United State less competitive in the global economy and add to an already bloated bureaucracy in Washington. Now let us examine some of the specific ways in which Obama will lead us down a more statist path.

# THE FEDERAL BUDGET: ENTITLEMENT PROGRAMS

The biggest problem facing the federal budget is entitlement spending. Simply based on the continuance of current trends, entitlements will soon make up most of the federal budget and leave very little money for the constitutional priorities of the federal government. The projections of future budget problems are frightening without even calculating what would happen if there were significant increases in the tax burden or benefits paid. Unfunded liabilities, or promises the federal government has made but not paid for, are already in the trillions of dollars.

The Social Security system is going bankrupt, because it is a bogus pyramid scheme by the federal government and because politicians like Obama have robbed the so-called "trust fund" for years. The money meant for retirement security has been spent on pet projects like the "bridge to nowhere" or a museum to commemorate the hippies at Woodstock. As the number of workers per retirees dwindles due to the demographic shift in this country, Social Security will go into the red around 2017 and be bankrupt by around 2040. As bad as that seems, Social Security is less of a financial disaster than Medicare, which remains a costly and ever-growing problem for the federal budget. The current system simply is not sustainable without fundamental reforms.

What does Senator Obama suggest we do about the entitlement crisis? Increase taxes without actually reforming the system, of course. Obama wants to increase taxes to generate more revenue for Social Security while at the same time he has voted against stopping the raid of the trust fund.[15] Instead of putting an end to the out-of-control spending in Congress that rewards special interests with earmarks, Obama wants to take more of our money to try and prop up the failing pyramid scheme of Social Security.

He is adamantly opposed to personal retirement accounts for younger workers, which would allow us to own, control and pass on our retirement money. In June of 2008, Obama stated that personal accounts would "gamble the retirement plans of millions of Americans on the stock market. That's why I stood up against this plan in the Senate, and that's why I won't stand for it as president."[16]

If Obama doesn't believe in the security and growth potential of the investment markets, he is ignoring a long history of wealth creation. Where does he think millions of 401(k) plans are invested? Spreading one's earnings out in mutual funds and individual retirement accounts is a much better deal than relying on government IOU's for your retirement. The personal account plans being proposed wouldn't take money from your grandparents, either; but they would allow younger workers to opt out of the system and begin to contribute their payroll tax dollars to a real retirement account so they can have their own "nest egg." Obama is using fear-mongering to scare people into relying upon the government for their retirement instead of relying on themselves and the growth engine of the world economy.

When given the opportunity to vote for "change" in Washington, Obama chose to support the status quo of raiding the Social Security trust fun for his own pet projects. For example, Obama has misspent federal funds on local projects like parks, museums and inner-city social programs.[17] Obama treats the treasury like a piggy bank for funding projects that benefit those who should be paying for these projects with local money. Like any good leftist, Obama believes that expanding federal government programs and securing money for local projects are great when you can make the taxpayers pay for them. For someone who talks about "change" so much, one would think that Obama could actually show some leadership on the entitlement crisis and earmark reform. But unfortunately, like a typical politician, he wants to kick the can down the road for future generations.

## OBAMA PROPOSES MORE ENTITLEMENTS

How else would Obama expand the federal government? Obama has promised everything to everyone, whether it is more taxpayer money for failing government schools in the U.S., or billions of dollars in foreign aid as part of his international social welfare scheme. Instead of asking Congress to tighten its belt and eliminate wasteful and duplicative programs, Obama wants to continue the trend of throwing more money at the bureaucrats to make everyone feel like they have accomplished something. An Obama presidency would mean less money in the taxpayers' wallets and more money in the hands of the federal government. Washington has a spending addiction, and Obama is ready to give the bureaucrats in charge of budgets yet another fix.

Obama would support a massive transfer of wealth from the private sector to the federal government, moving money from a productive sector to an unproductive sector. He will encourage the redistribution of trillions of dollars from the people that create jobs, goods and services, to the people that just collect paychecks and enforce burdensome rules and regulations. All of this money will be confiscated from hard-working Americans so that the politicians and bureaucrats can redistribute it to wasteful programs. This will have a lasting impact on our economy and discourage economic growth, individual creativity, and job creation in the U.S.

## MORE TAXES, MORE SPENDING

When asked how he will pay for all his favorite government monstrosities, Obama replies that he will (1) use the money from the repeal of the Bush tax cuts and (2) spend the money saved from ending the war in Iraq in order to spend it on his domestic priorities. It is questionable whether or not this financial redistribution would be able to "pay" for his favorite programs, but more important is the effect his tax hikes would have on our economy.

Repealing the Bush tax relief would amount to trillions of dollars in new taxes at a time when confidence in the American economy is waning. Raising taxes on businesses, families and investors would not only make us poorer, but it would provide a disincentive to invest in businesses and thereby create new jobs. The biggest engines of job creation in America are our small businesses. What liberals like Obama refuse to admit is that many of the folks that are in the top 10% income tax bracket are small business owners who file as individuals. Are these the super wealthy fat-cats that Obama wants to target for more monetary confiscation? Apparently so. Despite the fact that the top 10% of income earners pay more than 68% of the nation's taxes, Obama wants to punish them with an even more burdensome load.[18]

Let's set the record straight on who pays most of the taxes. If you look at the top 25% of income earners, they pay more than 85% of the taxes to the federal government. And if you look at the bottom 50% of income earners in this country, they pay only 3% of the income taxes.[19] As economist Steve Moore points out, the wealthy actually pay a *larger* share of the taxes under the Bush administration's tax cuts of 2001 and 2003 than they did before the tax cuts went into effect.[20] But the left believes that "the rich" should pay much more, even if that means a lot of small businesses will feel the pain. Class warfare rhetoric on taxes has poisoned the debate and obscured the facts about who bears the burden, and who doesn't. And Obama has been one of the most vocal purveyors of this kind of misleading populist rhetoric.

What effects will Obama's tax hikes have on our economy? Capital flows where it is treated positively, not where it is treated negatively. People do not invest in an area when they know the government will take most of the profit. That is why so much money and investment has been flowing to states like Texas and not Michigan. Texas has no state income tax and has a generally pro-business climate, while Michigan has tried to tax and regulate its way to prosperity, failing miserably. Capital is also flowing to countries in Eastern Europe where tax competition is underway. While Slovakia, Estonia and the Czech Republic are passing a flat tax to attract investments and encourage economic growth, the Presidential nominee for the Democrat Party in the United States is pushing for higher taxes on American businesses and families.

As Steve Moore pointed out in a column in 2007, freedom is on the march in many places, but not necessarily in the U.S.[21] Now would be the worst time to move us in the direction of higher taxes and other anti-capital policies. If we do not make some major adjustments, European and Asian financial centers will become more important than our own financial centers. In the *flat* world of the globalizing 21st century, making your own country less competitive is a dangerous and disturbing proposition. It is unfortunate that Obama has taken such an anti-market stance, both rhetorically and in his votes in the Senate. The next president will need to support policies that prepare the U.S. for the 21$^{st}$ century economy. Obama does not seem to have the economic knowledge necessary to make that happen. Instead, he seems to be enamored with the policies of President Jimmy Carter from the 1970s. We simply cannot afford a second term for Jimmy Carter in this country.

Because the repeal of the Bush tax cuts will not satiate Obama's desire to tax and spend, he has also voted for a Senate Democrat budget proposal that would add more taxes on the backs of middle class Americans, the same people that he claims to care so much about. If these tax hikes are passed this year, those making as little as $31,850 a year could see their taxes rise at a time when the cost of living is also rising.[22]

And if that was not enough punishment, Obama does not support a full repeal of either the alternative minimum tax or the death tax.[23] The AMT was supposed to be a tax on a very small percentage of the wealthy, but because it was not adjusted for inflation it could hit as many as 23 million Americans. The death tax, euphemistically called the estate tax, is an especially egregious type of taxation *after* one passes away. This redistribution scheme is a way for greedy politicians to get their hands on more money after a person dies. Not only is a death tax an example of double taxation, but it can be quite a burden on families who inherit the estate and have to pay the taxes when their loved one dies. Unless Congress acts, the death tax relief passed in 2001 will revert back to its previous levels of an outrageous 60% on some estates.

This kind of government theft of money is simply counter to the limited government principles that America was founded on. It punishes wealth creation, savings and investment, and represents the kind of collectivist thinking that motivates the left. Recent Congressional Democrat budgets have repeatedly calculated the revenues generated by the AMT and the expiration of the death tax relief in their projections, and Obama has happily supported these budgets. So much for trying to make people's lives better. This is yet another example where Obama's rhetoric and actions are in conflict. Increasing taxes on the middle class and business owners does not give them much "hope" for the future.

## ENERGY POLICY: ENVIRONMENTALISM AND TAXATION

A tax and spend liberal like Obama would not be complete without a dose of fierce anti-corporate policy proposals. Because Obama has a disdain for the dreaded oil companies, he has supported a "windfall profits tax" and a "cap and trade" system. Obama should talk to his political precursor Jimmy Carter about the disaster that was the windfall profits tax, beginning in the late 1970s. Thankfully, Carter's bad policy was finally repealed in 1988, but now the idea is back with a vengeance.

Senator Dick Durbin, an Obama supporter and fellow Illinois Senator, commented recently, "The oil companies need to know that there is a limit on how much profit they can take in this economy."[24] The Senate Democrat proposal would tax anything considered to be an "unreasonable profit" at 25% unless the oil companies invest in the "alternative energy" companies that support the Democrat Party. This kind of tax is merely a populist political gimmick that channels the irrational hatred of oil and gas companies for political gain for the politicians calling for the tax.

The left always fails to explain what "unreasonable profits" are. Perhaps the liberal politicians make too much and we should set a windfall profits tax on their salaries and impose a windfall tax on them when they sell their mansions. The rhetoric is absurd, and so is the policy. The last time this was tried, domestic production decreased and our imports of energy increased. The windfall tax would have the effect of raising energy prices, not lowering them. Still Senator Obama's Democrat colleagues voted for the tax in June 2008. Obama didn't show up for the vote, but stated publicly many times that he supports the policy.[25]

As for the leftist paranoia on climate change, the latest craze is a so-called "cap and trade" scheme that will ostensibly allow "the rise of the oceans to slow" and the planet to heal. At least this is how we can interpret Obama's messianic speech upon winning the Democrat nomination for president.[26] Unfortunately for Obama, the costs of quixotically attacking climate change will be more than our economy can bear.

The Congressional Budget Office (CBO) estimates that a cap and trade system would add billions of dollars to the price of energy. Cap and trade is a scheme whereby the government sets a cap on allowable carbon emissions and companies that stay under the cap can trade their credits to companies that go over the limit. But as the CBO points out, such a system would disproportionately harm the poor, cost Americans hundreds of thousands of jobs and discourage energy production.[27]

With the price of oil and gas rising steadily, adding to the cost of filling our gas tanks is not a good idea. But Obama seems sanguine about the prospects of rising gas prices. He was quoted in June 2008 as saying, "I think that I would have preferred a gradual adjustment." I doubt that going on record in support of gradually increasing gas prices will play well in middle America. Perhaps that is why Obama supports "cap and trade" – he is in favor of anything that makes the "evil" oil and gas companies pass on higher costs to consumers.

Punishing oil and gas companies has another way of hurting the average American worker. As Ben Stein points out, tens of millions of Americans depend upon the productivity and success of American oil companies like Exxon-Mobil. Our 401(k) plans and pensions are heavily invested in American companies, including oil companies that seek to turn a profit for their shareholders. As Stein argues, Exxon-Mobil actually has more small investors than big investors.[28]

Attacking big corporations is a typical tactic of the left to rile up their union base and ignite class warfare against those labeled wealthy and greedy. The fact that raising taxes on oil and gas companies will take money out of the pockets of middle class Americans is lost on liberals like Obama. What really matters is that big businesses are punished for being successful and turning a profit. It does not matter to them that oil companies actually have a smaller profit margin (around 7-9%) than most other industries.

While Obama claims he wants to detach us from our dependency on foreign oil, he is opposed to domestic exploration for energy.[29] Given the rising costs of fuel, the national security implications of foreign dependence on oil, and the economic boost this would give the economy, it is hard to understand why Obama would not support more domestic energy exploration. Perhaps he is pandering to radical anti-energy environmentalists, but that is a poor excuse for making American consumers feel more pain at the pump. It will be hard to explain to the American people why he refuses to increase the supply of energy, while also increasing taxes on energy production. Both of these policies drive up the price of gas, which is not something that is too popular these days.

## MORE GOVERNMENT REGULATION OF INDUSTRY

Obama has joined the chorus of Democrat candidates John Edwards and Hillary Clinton in bashing other entire industries, including pharmaceutical companies, insurance providers and health care providers. This is not to say that these companies have not done things that justify some righteous indignation, but the rhetorical vitriol goes beyond helpful criticism or oversight and borders on Marxist demagoguery.

We can only conclude that the rhetoric would become policy if Obama were elected president, given his past votes in the Senate on taxation and regulation. If so, what would such policies do to improve the availability and quality of pharmaceuticals, insurance or health care in this country? Would a government takeover of these industries improve the situation? What would be the effects of the market distortions created by government regulations and meddling? Obama and his liberal friends have not seriously considered these questions. Obama uses this rhetoric as a way to throw some red meat to the populist, neo-Marxist elements of the Democrat party base during his many oratorical performances.

Not content to increase taxes and spending on American companies and families, Obama also wants to return us to the age of protectionism. While we are making the U.S. less competitive globally, we might as well add a pinch of backward trade policy to the mix, right? His now-famous NAFTA bashing in Ohio even worried Canadian officials to the point where Obama's aides had to reassure the Canadians that Obama was just pandering to voters in Ohio and thus, not to worry.[30]

The North American Free Trade Agreement (NAFTA) has been a net benefit for Canada, the U.S. and Mexico. Yes, some jobs have been lost, but others have been gained. Such is the nature of a changing and vibrant economic exchange between free peoples. Free trade has been proven *ad nauseum* to benefit everyone in the long run. But economic shortsightedness and class warfare pervade the Democrat party and its water-carriers, the unions. Therefore, Obama has had to talk tough on American companies that "move jobs overseas" to places that cost less to do business. He has sounded defiant on current trade deals in Congress, including with Peru, Panama, Colombia and South Korea. He says that he will not support trade deals unless they include provisions on labor and environmental standards that meet his criteria.[31]

These deals actually do have standards that should satisfy Obama, but he continues to oppose them despite the opportunity the deals would provide to our friends in Latin America and elsewhere. Closing the U.S. market to the world for foreign investment and erecting trade barriers reeks of the close-minded and autarkic mindset of the "economic nationalists." Adam Smith long ago (1776) pointed out the benefits of trade, but apparently the *Wealth of Nations* is not on the Columbia University reading list.

Why is the Democrat party's leader rejecting the positive work of President Bill Clinton on NAFTA instead of embracing his legacy? The answer given to the Canadian representatives indicates that Obama was simply pandering to a group of voters for short-term political gain. If this is the answer, then so much for the politics of "change" that Obama promised to bring to Washington. It sounds more like the same old politics. If Obama really does believe in re-negotiating trade deals and installing barriers to a free exchange of goods across borders, then perhaps he just does not understand economics. Either way, his public statements on the issue add to the doubts about his quest to be a trustworthy leader or a good steward of the American economy.

Barack Obama peddles a message of "hope" to the American people. But his policies would deflate the hopes and dreams of millions of Americans that rely on a strong economy for good jobs, real retirement security and money to spend on vacations, hobbies and whatever else their hearts desire. As my boss Dick Armey says, "Being ignorant of economics seems to be a prerequisite to becoming a Democrat." Whether it is ignorance of economics, political pandering, or a misplaced infatuation with statism, Obama's plans for our economy would be disastrous to individuals, families and businesses. He would add to our growing debt by expanding entitlement programs and redistributing trillions of dollars of wealth from the American people to the federal government. Under a President Obama, the wealth creating private sector would lose power and influence and the wealth confiscating government sector would increase.

Americans cherish our economic liberty and the idea that you should keep what you earn by the sweat of your brow. But Obama's massive redistribution scheme and big government credo require that Americans give up more of what they earn to pay for a federal government that is already too enormous and foolishly spends the money it receives. The bottom line is that Obama would implement higher taxes, more government regulation and less economic freedom. This comes at a time when the American economy is on shaky ground and we need a president who will support lower taxes, less government and more freedom. It is up to the American people to choose a president that believes in free enterprise and competition, not one whose ideas are based on the growth of government and the punishment of hard-working Americans.

15  http://www.opencongress.org/people/voting_history/400629_barack_obama

16  Mark Niquette, "Obama has plan for senior citizens," *The Columbus Dispatch*, http://www.dispatch.com/live/content/local_news/stories/2008/06/13/obamahere.html?sid=101#Scene_1, (13 June 2008).

17  Obama earmark request FY 2006 and FY 2007, http://answercenter.barackobama.com/cgi-bin/barackobama.cfg/php/enduser/std_adp.php?p_faqid=172&p_created=1205426026&p_sid=TNlxoC-i&p_accessibility=0&p_redirect=&p_lva=&p_sp=cF9zcmNoPTEmcF9zb3J0X2J5PSZwX2dyaWRzb3J0PSZwX3Jvd19jbnQ9MSwxJnBfcHJvZHM9JnBfY2F0cz (released 13 March 2008 on Obama's campaign website).

18  Stephen Moore, "Guess Who Really Pays the Taxes", *The American*, http://www.american.com/archive/2007/november-december-magazine-contents/guess-who-really-pays-the-taxes, (November/December 2007).

19  Ibid.

20  Ibid.

21  Stephen Moore, "The Supply-Side Solution: If tax-cut strategies don't work, why are they so popular abroad?" *The Wall Street Journal*, http://opinionjournal.com/extra/?id=110010844, (9 November 2007).

22  Associated Press, "Presidential contenders back at Capitol to vote on tax bills," *Boston Herald*, http://news.bostonherald.com/news/2008/view.bg?articleid=1080173, (14 March 2008).

23  http://www.ontheissues.org/Economic/Barack_Obama_Tax_Reform.htm

24  H. Josef Hebert, "Senate debates windfall profits tax on oil", *Washington Times*, http://www.washingtontimes.com/news/2008/jun/10/senate-debates-windfall-profits-tax-on-oil/, (9 June 2008).

[25]   United States Senate, H.R. 6049, Renewable Energy and Job Creation Act of 2008, http://www.senate.gov/legislative/LIS/roll_call_lists/roll_call_vote_cfm.cfm?congress=110&session=2&vote=00147, roll call, (10 June 2008).

[26]   Campaign speech, St. Paul, MN, "Remarks of Senator Obama," http://www.barackobama.com/2008/06/03/remarks_of_senator_barack_obam_73.php, (3 June 2008).

[27]   Congressional Budget Office, http://www.cbo.gov/ftpdocs/80xx/doc8027/04-25-Cap_Trade.pdf .

[28]   Ben Stein, "Exxon Mobil Needs a Hug," *New York Times*, http://www.nytimes.com/2008/03/02/business/02every.html?_r=1&oref=slogin&pagewanted=all (2 March 2008).

[29]   Shailagh Murray, "Clinton-Obama Differences Clear in Senate Votes," *Washington Post*, http://www.washingtonpost.com/wp-dyn/content/article/2006/12/31/AR2006123101004.html, (1 January 2007).

[30]   Michael van der Galien, "Obama Flip-Flops on NAFTA," *Real Clear Politics*, http://www.realclearpolitics.com/cross_tabs/2008/06/obama_flipflops_on_nafta.html, (19 June 2008).

[31]   Brian Montopoli, "Obama's Balancing Act on Free Trade," http://www.cbsnews.com/stories/2008/06/20/politics/main4198107.shtml, (20 June 2008).

# CHAPTER 3

## FROM MEDICAL TAPE TO RED TAPE:
## BARACK OBAMA ON HEALTH CARE AND SOCIALIZED
## MEDICINE

At the forefront of American politics today is the debate over health insurance and health care. Barack Obama has established himself as a candidate on the far left and pledged for more government control of the health care system. Touting a plan of "universal health care," Obama's plan will create more government bureaucracy and foster more failed government policies. He has attempted to reshape, repackage and reproduce it to be something other than what it really is—a program more fit for the Soviet Union of the 1970's than for the United States of America of today.

During his eight years in the Illinois State Senate as well as his brief tenure as US Senator, Obama championed socialized medicine and sponsored legislation to implement it. Determined to enact a far left agenda, Obama continues to spout his radical ideals as he campaigns for President of the United States. Perhaps the best way to analyze Barack Obama's feelings on this subject is to revisit a speech he gave while campaigning in May of 2007. His speech touched on each major point of his health care platform, and unveiled other deeply rooted beliefs of which Americans were undoubtedly unaware. By reading his speech, we gain a better understanding of Barack Obama's stance on health care and his desire to bring the United States one step closer to socialism.

# AMERICANS ARE HAPPY WITH THEIR HEALTHCARE

After thanking the University of Iowa for hosting him, Obama relayed a story of a supporter who had battled through health problems. He then began:

> We are not a country that rewards hard work and
> perseverance with bankruptcies and foreclosures. We are
> not a country that allows major challenges to go unsolved
> and unaddressed while our people suffer needlessly. In
> the richest nation on Earth, it is simply not right that the
> skyrocketing profits of the drug and insurance industries
> are paid for by the skyrocketing premiums that come from
> the pockets of the American people. This is not who we
> are. And this is not who we have to be. [32]

Obama immediately attacked private companies, and set the stage for a speech on the benefits of socialized medicine. On the campaign trail, Obama has joined with the far left in reiterating the false belief that all of America is frustrated with their health care. Barack Obama would have you believe that Americans are unhappy with their health care coverage and want a drastic change.

Unfortunately for Barack Obama that is not the case. A poll conduced by CBS News only three months prior to Obama's speech indicates otherwise. When asked, "Would government do better or worse at providing coverage than private companies" 44% indicated "the government would do worse." Only 30% believed "the government would do better," 24% of those surveyed did not know.[33]

Obama claims major challenges are going unsolved and Americans are suffering needlessly. Again, we find that just the opposite is true. According to the same CBS poll, 77% of Americans were satisfied with their health care while only 20% were dissatisfied.[34] Despite Obama's erroneous claim an overwhelming number of Americans are satisfied with the quality of health care they are receiving.

# Obama Worked With Lobbyists

> In the past few months, I've heard stories… from people who are hanging on by a thread because of the stack of medical bills they can't pay… People who watch as every year, candidates offer up detailed health care plans with great fanfare and promise, only to see them crushed under the weight of Washington politics and drug and insurance industry lobbying once the campaign is over.[35]

Here Barack Obama makes an accusation commonly used by politicians today. When all else fails, blame the special interests, and their greedy lobbyists. Obama has campaigned for President on the platform of fighting the special interests, claiming that lobbyists are harming our nation by driving up prices and taking advantage of hardworking Americans. An examination of his time in the Illinois State Senate tells a different story though. While serving in the legislature Barack Obama accepted money from both the insurance companies and those who lobbied on their behalf. These donations included $1,000 from the Illinois Insurance PAC and the Professional Independent Insurance Agents PAC. [36]

In addition to accepting money, Obama also earned the praise of lobbyists throughout the state of Illinois. Phil Lackman, a lobbyist specializing in work for the insurance companies said, "Barack is a very reasonable person who clearly recognized the various roles involved in the healthcare system." [37] Barack Obama's proclamations of "change" fall flat when challenged on the facts. Contrary to the image he has attempted to create for himself, he stands with far left politicians of the day willing to side step the truth in exchange for a campaign victory.

## The Rising Cost of Insurance Premiums

> We have reached a point in this country where the rising cost of health care has put too many families and businesses on a collision course with financial ruin and left too many without coverage at all… Health care premiums have risen nearly 90% in the past six years…[38]

Again we see that Obama is more than content to be erratic with his facts and figures. Obama's claim that insurance premiums rose nearly 90% is misleading. According to its annual Employer Health Benefits Survey, the Kaiser Family Foundation reported that premiums for family coverage have risen since 2001. The rise in insurance premiums however was only about 78% for family coverage and not "nearly 90%" as Barack Obama claimed. [39] Obama's willingness to exaggerate numbers to sway his audience is apparent. He prefers to prey on emotion to manipulate the audience to believe his agenda. In other instances, the problem lies not with Barack Obama's false statistics, but his inept logic.

## WHO IS RESPONSIBLE FOR RISING COSTS?

> Over half of all small businesses can no longer afford to insure their workers, and so many others have responded to rising costs by laying off workers or shutting their doors for good. Some of the biggest corporations in America, giants of industry like GM and Ford, are watching foreign competitors based in countries with universal health care run circles around them, with a GM car containing seven times as much health care cost as a Japanese car. [40]

Obama's logic is inherently flawed. His assumption that universal care will lead to lower cost and better service is one of the greatest mistruths to be spread by the left. John Stossel, best selling author and anchor of ABC's *20/20* sees it differently. "The biggest problem with insurance is that it increases nasty incentives," he says. "It encourages us to spend more and not to think about what things cost. What if your car insurance covered oil changes and gasoline? You wouldn't care how much gas you use and you wouldn't care what it cost. Mechanics would sell you hundred dollar oil changes." [41]

The cost of health care rises when we resort to socialized medicine. The cost does not go down, as Barack Obama would have you believe. Without a need to be responsible, some will visit the doctor excessively. When someone knows his insurance will pick up the tab, a simple cold or fever becomes a doctor visit, a medical bill, and a rise in premiums for Americans. Stossel continues, "That's how it works in health care, and some people demand 'oil changes' whether they need them or not... What if you had grocery insurance? You wouldn't care what things cost. Why by hamburger? I'll just buy steak." [42]

## MORE GOVERNMENT REGULATION LEADS TO INEFFICIENCY

> It would be one thing if all this money we spend on premiums and co-payments and deductibles went directly towards making us healthier and improving the quality of our care. But it doesn't... Each year, 100,000 Americans die due to medical errors and we lose $100 billion because of prescription drug errors alone. [43]

While not factually incorrect, Obama's statement is directly at odds with the free market system our nation was founded upon. The framers of the Constitution understood that limiting government intervention was the surest way to provide for a strong and vibrant economy. When restrictions are placed on businesses those organizations are unable to meet the demands for new technology and better products. When tax hikes are implemented, those businesses no longer have an incentive to innovate and create better and more efficient ways to work. In the American health care system, the endless levels of bureaucracy attribute to a lack of innovation and lead to an increase in illness and death.

The Food and Drug Administration (FDA), was established in 1906 and is an agency of the Department of Health and Human Services. The FDA is responsible for some successes, such as ensuring that products remain unspoiled and that contaminated food is not sold to customers. When bureaucrats like Barack Obama urge government to do more however, we see its true nature begin to show. Picture an administrator for the FDA arriving at a press conference and stating, "After 10 years of research we have finally approved a new blood pressure medication. This year 10,000 people's lives will be saved."

It sounds good in theory but consider that stream of logic. If next year 10,000 people will be saved due to the drug's approval, then it means last year 10,000 people died while waiting for the drug to be given the green light. It means over the past five years 50,000 people died waiting for its release and since the drug's initial testing, 100,000 people died waiting for it to be approved by the government. Those people would have been better off trying an experimental drug or taking the drug without FDA approval. As with many government agencies, the FDA is a bureaucratic agency run amok. [44]

## GOVERNMENT REGULATION LEADS TO NEEDLESS DEATH

> We also spend far more on treating illnesses and conditions that could've been prevented or managed for far less. Our health care system is turning into a disease care system, where too many plans and providers don't offer or encourage check-ups and tests and screenings that could save thousands of lives and billions of dollars down the road.[45]

Barack Obama would have you believe that private businesses and drug companies contribute to higher costs and the loss of lives. He believes that companies and insurance agencies aren't providing adequate care in an effort to make more money. Once again we see that Obama's big government ideology directly influences his beliefs on how to reform the health care system. It is that ideology that hurts individuals who need new drugs to be developed to ease their pain or save their life.

A number of organizations were established throughout the country in response to the growing frustration against the FDA and government bureaucracy. Life Extension Foundation, a non-profit based out of Florida has the expressed goal of aiding in "the radical extension of the healthy human lifespan." The organization examines ways to improve quality of life and seeks out methods of treatment overlooked by government agencies.

In August of 2003, Life Extension Magazine wrote about a new drug that seemed to be effective against ovarian cancer, a disease that kills approximately 15,000 women each year. Just three months prior, the Yale University School of Medicine announced that the drug, phenoxodiol, had induced a 100% death rate in cancer cells, including even those cells proven resistant to chemotherapy drugs. [46]

It would be another year and a half before the FDA decided to grant fast-track status to phenoxodiol, enabling it to take the next step towards federal approval. Though the FDA acknowledged the drug demonstrated a possibility for success, phenoxodiol has yet to be approved for use. An increasing government bureaucracy has prevented private organizations from continuing to develop this drug and use it to save American live. It has been almost four years since the FDA approved further research for the drug.

## How Much is Too Much?

> Since President Bush took office, the single fastest growing component of health care spending has been administrative costs and profits for insurance companies... In 2006, five of the biggest drug and insurance companies were among the fifty most profitable businesses in the nation. One insurance company CEO received a $125 million salary that same year, and has been given stock options worth over $1 billion. As an added perk, he and his wife get free private health care for as long as they live. [47]

While a discussion of, "how much is enough?" could serve as its own chapter, one wonders what right those on the left have to determine the wages or benefits set by a private business. Rarely do we hear politicians and those on the left lamenting over the salaries of NBA basketball players, Hollywood actors, or rock and roll musicians. So then why does a private business fall under a different category? Curiously, Barack Obama criticizes CEOs for their exorbitant salary while perhaps he should question if he himself is making too much money. According to Obama's tax returns released in March of 2008, he made more than $500,000 in author fees from his book, *The Audacity of Hope* in the year 2006 alone, more than 10 times the yearly income of the average American family. [48]

## OBAMA'S EXPLOITS IN THE ILLINOIS STATE SENATE

> As a state senator, I brought Republicans and Democrats together to pass legislation insuring 20,000 more children and 65,000 more parents… And I passed a law that put Illinois on a path to universal coverage. [49]

No speech by Barack Obama would be complete without a reference to his purported successes in the Illinois State Senate. With fewer than four years in the United States Senate and few accomplishments to speak of, Obama relies time and again on his years as a state legislator. The law Obama was referring to was HB2268, the "Health Care Justice Act." Co-sponsored by Obama in the Senate and signed into law in August of 2004, the act originally called for a plan to grant care to the more than 12 million residents of the state. [50]

The cost to the taxpayers of Illinois would be so excessive, there was doubt even from those within the government that the state could afford it without a federal subsidy. The cost would be so outlandish that the Department of Public Aid included a fiscal note to the legislation stating, "There could be substantial and prohibitive costs when the final report is released. The bill does not contain any estimate of the future costs of comprehensive health care in Illinois. Last year, we estimated the cost of this proposal could be between $2.6 billion and $4 billion annually. It is doubtful the Department could finance a comprehensive health care program without federal participation, especially given the current state of the State's fiscal condition." [51]

Despite his tough talk on the campaign trail against lobbyists, Obama's actions at the time were anything but. As the debate continued, Obama took steps to make the bill more favorable to health care insurers. Universal health care itself was relegated to a mere goal instead of actual state policy. The "Adequate Health Care Task Force" was established and charged only with studying how to expand health care access, rather than actually implementing it.

Barack Obama strives to rip apart the foundational principles upon which our nation was formed. With Barack Obama's ideology leading the way, the United States would begin to turn on its philosophy of liberty and its free market system.

## There is No Mistaking Obama's Objective

> The very first promise I made on this campaign was that as president, I will sign a universal health care plan into law by the end of my first term in office… My plan begins by covering every American. If you already have health insurance, the only thing that will change for you under this plan is the amount of money you will spend on premiums. That will be less.[52]

Make no mistake about the motives of Barack Obama. As a part of the far left it is his goal to institute socialized medicine throughout the United States. Supporters sometimes claim that Obama does not truly believe in socialism and that such charges are meritless attacks by his opponents. Do not be fooled by the rhetoric of Barack Obama and other big government advocates. "Universal health care" is the left's codeword for socialized medicine. It exemplifies the failure of government involvement in what should be private institutions. Obama promises that Americans with insurance would see no change and actually save money. This claim is simply false.

Families USA, an organization focused on helping Americans achieve high-quality, affordable health care, states that the cost of providing care for the uninsured is one of the major reasons the cost of premiums increases. A report in June of 2005 by Families USA states that the average American family pays more than $900 in premiums due to cost of care for those without insurance. [53]

In some places a $900 increase in premiums would be a welcome cost, preferable to what some states are enduring now. Families USA says, "In six states health insurance premiums for families are at least $1,500 higher due to the unreimbursed cost of health care for the uninsured in 2005."

| | |
|---|---|
| New Mexico | $1,875 |
| West Virginia | $1,796 |
| Oklahoma | $1,781 |
| Montana | $1,578 |
| Texas | $1,551 |
| Arkansas | $1,514 [54] |

Despite the high premiums being paid by those with insurance, they are still only partially covering the cost of those without coverage. The study states, "More than one-third of the total cost of health care services provided to people without health insurance is paid out-of-pocket by the uninsured themselves." [55] If Barack Obama successfully initiates a program of socialized medicine where would the revenue for the additional two-thirds come from? That's right, the American taxpayer.

## HOW TO INSURE 20 MILLION AMERICANS IN TWO MINUTES

> If you are one of the 45 million Americans who don't have health insurance, you will have it after this plan becomes law…[56]

Perhaps the most often quoted and thereby misleading statistic in Barack Obama's speeches on health insurance is the sheer number of people in America who currently have no coverage. As with many of his other facts, these twisted numbers are misleading Americans looking for honest figures in the health care debate. Upon further research we find the supposed health care "crisis" Barack Obama is exploiting, simply does not exist.

According to the US Census Bureau's 2005 report on "Income, Poverty, and Health Insurance Coverage," the number of Americans without insurance is 47 million. Any marks for Barack Obama's honesty end there however. A closer look at the Census report finds that of the 47 million listed as not having insurance, more than nine million are not American citizens. [57] Somehow Barack Obama ignores this fact as he pushes his agenda to advocate socialized medicine. Taking this into account the number drops to approximately 38 million people without health insurance.

Of those now remaining, almost nine million additional individuals make over $75,000 a year, nearly double the median household income of $46,326. [58] It stands to reason that if they desire it, these individuals should be able to afford health insurance. Adjusting for that factor and the number slides to approximately 29 million.

With this new number of uninsured, roughly eight million people make between $50,000 and $75,000 a year. [59] Though family size and personal expenses are clearly different in every situation, this amount is still more than the median household income of the typical American family. These individuals should be able to afford health insurance if they choose to purchase it. This drops the number even further to just over 20 million people. In the two-minute time span it took you to read the above paragraphs, we've lowered the number of "uninsured Americans" in this country by 27 million. Now that is change that would make even Barack Obama jealous.

And yet the "new" number of 20 million uninsured Americans may even be too high. Dr. David Gratzer believes the overall statistics are inflated because a number of American citizens freely choose not to get insurance. Citing a study commissioned by the California Healthcare Foundation on individuals, at least 200% above the federal poverty line but still without insurance, he says, "Many Americans are uninsured by choice... Why the lack of insurance? One clue is that 60 percent reported being in excellent health or very good health." [60]

We see that some Americans do not have health insurance by choice. A strong case could be made for young individuals in excellent health to forego insurance and place the money they would have spent into investments. An able bodied 25-year-old with no history of disease does not need the same care, nor pose the same risk of illness, as someone in their late 80s or 90s.

The number of true "uninsured" Americans could perhaps be lowered again with the estimation that almost half of those uninsured will have insurance within four months. According to the Congressional Budget office, many individuals are not covered due to transitional periods between jobs. As many people receive insurance through their employer, they would be covered upon taking the new position. It is estimated that 45% of those without insurance will have it within four months. [61]

Is there actually a "crisis" when it comes to American citizens and their inability to obtain health insurance? In a word, "No." The media and politicians like Barack Obama continue to harp on the need for socialized medicine, even though the number of Americans who are unable to get insurance is drastically lower than what Barack Obama would have you believe. So where do the exact numbers stand? There is no way to be certain, although some estimates put the number as low as eight million people; [62] a significant difference from the 47 million people the proponents of big government would have you believe.

In his zeal to push his radical leftist agenda, Obama is quick to talk and slow to listen. The faulty numbers he provides on the campaign trail grossly mischaracterize a situation that should be addressed openly and honestly. In many cases he capitalized on the misconceptions by the public and used those fallacies to his advantage.

# Is U.S. Health Care Inferior to the Rest of the World?

> But we also have to demand greater efficiencies from our
> health care system. Today, we pay almost twice as much for
> health care per person than other industrialized nations,
> and too much of it has nothing to do with patient care. [63]

One of the major arguments used by the left is the substantial cost of health care in the United States as compared to other industrialized countries, mainly Canada and Europe. Advocates of socialized medicine constantly assert the superiority of other nations over the US based on the belief that health care is so inexpensive to citizens of these countries. Many on the left even claim that health care in those countries is "free."

The argument falls flat because there is nothing "free" about it. Barack Obama's praise for the low cost of health care in other nations is hollow when the facts are brought to light. In France the health care system is suffering a number of shortfalls while the means of collecting revenue is often hidden. Michael D. Tanner, senior fellow at the Cato Institute writes, "It's funded through a 13.55 percent payroll tax, a 5.25 percent income tax and other taxes on tobacco, alcohol and drug-company revenues. And the system is still running a $15.6 billion deficit." [64]

In the United Kingdom we see more of the same; perceived low cost with hidden expenses that increase price and decrease quality. The UK's National Health Service serves as a reminder of what can happen when competition begins to fade and socialized medicine takes over. Barack Obama would have you believe that things are better elsewhere, but columnist Giles Whitt of the Times of London sees it differently. He writes, "It goes without saying that healthcare on the NHS isn't free. But just how un-free it is gets too little attention. We pay for it through our noses, every month. Next year's NHS budget will be about £104 billion. That's roughly £1,733 per man, woman and child. Multiplied by four for a typical two-child family, then divided by 12, that equates to median monthly family healthcare expenditure of £577, or $1,155 in

American money. I can buy some very respectable US health insurance for $1,155 a month." [65] Just like his campaign, Obama's "facts" are based on emotion. When put to the test they fall apart. While speaking to the crowd in Iowa Obama unveiled the five-part plan he alleged would lower costs and improve the quality of health care.

## FOREIGN CITIZENS COME TO THE U.S. FOR CARE

> First, we will reduce costs for business and their workers by picking up the tab for some of the most expensive illnesses and conditions… Patients with serious illnesses like cancer or heart disease whom require the most expensive surgeries and treatments. Under my proposal, the federal government will pay for part of these catastrophic cases, which means that your premiums will go down.[66]

The immediate question (once again) is where this money would come from. Politicians often present solutions to problems by claiming the federal government will take care of it, as if the federal government is a separate entity operating on another planet. The underlying message is that Barack Obama will raise taxes.

Under Barack Obama's plan for socialized medicine he claims the government will pick up the bill for patients suffering from serious ailments such as cancer or heart disease. According to his program this would decrease premiums, lowers costs, and increase the quality of care. Barack Obama seems to be living on the same planet he envisions the federal government resides.

Time after time foreign celebrities and leaders leave their home countries when they need serious medical care and travel to the United States to reap the benefits of free market choices. In Canada, the health care idol of the left, government control actually hurts citizens who need serious procedures performed. Many times the government delays or even refuses to offer care based upon how necessary they deem the procedure to be.

Shirley Healey, a Canadian citizen, was suffering from a blocked artery that was keeping her from digesting food. Though she had already lost nearly 50 pounds, the Canadian health care system called her surgery "elective" and refused to cover it. Frustrated by the government run system and suffering the effects of her illness, Shirley decided to leave Canada and travel to the United States. There she saw an American doctor in Washington State who performed the surgery right away, informing Shirley she would only have a few weeks to live without immediate medical attention. When asked if she felt taken advantage of by an American system that critics claimed was driven only by greed, Healy said, "The idea of somebody profiting, who cares? I'm alive and I really don't care. That's the only part that's important to me." [67]

## HEALTH *INSURANCE* DOES NOT EQUAL HEALTH *CARE*

> Second, we will finally begin focusing our health care
> system on preventing costly, debilitating conditions in
> the first place... The real profit today is made in treating
> diseases, not preventing them. That's wrong, which
> is why in our new national health care plan and other
> participating plans, we will require coverage of evidence-
> based, preventive care services, and make sure they are paid
> for.[68]

Obama stumbled upon a truth at this point in his speech, though any hope for him to realize the error of his ways is quickly dashed. Preventative care is indeed more effective than treating people who are already sick. Individuals who eat right, get enough sleep, and get daily exercise end up living longer, healthier lives. But Barack Obama misses the point, as does the rest of the far left. While they applaud socialized medicine and the universal coverage it supposedly brings to its citizens, they refuse to admit where they themselves would go for care if affected by a serious illness.

Michael Tanner and Michael Cannon of the CATO Institute explain some of the misconceptions regarding health insurance. "Simply saying that people have health insurance is meaningless," they write. "Many countries provide universal insurance but deny critical procedures to patients who need them. Britain's Department of Health reported in 2006 that at any given time, nearly 900,000 Britons are waiting for admission to National Health Service hospitals, and shortages force the cancellation of more than 50,000 operations each year." [69]

Advocates of big government solutions fail to realize that giving Americans coverage is vastly different than actually providing them with the care they need in crucial times. When government controls health care, it is the government that determines who will be treated first based upon the regulations the government imposes. Patients stop being individuals with real lives and real families and start becoming numbers in a ranked database.

CATO's Tanner and Cooper caution proponents of universal health care to be wary of the quick fix solutions proposed by some politicians and urge them to examine the facts before they advocate for government controlled medicine. They write, "In Sweden, the wait for heart surgery can be as long as 25 weeks, and the average wait for hip replacement surgery is more than a year. Many of these individuals suffer chronic pain, and judging by the numbers, some will probably die awaiting treatment." [70]

One of the biggest lies used by leftists like Barack Obama is that the United States is suffering a shortage of health care. Contrary to popular myths spread by the left, there is no shortage of health care in the US. In fact every American has access to health care in the case of Emergency Room service. Hospitals are legally required to provide care regardless of whether or not the patient can provide payment. What all Americans do not necessarily have is health insurance; though the question we should be asking is not how to get all Americans insurance, but whether or not all Americans need insurance.

Though some Americans lack health insurance, it has not yet been proven that having health insurance guarantees a patient better health care. A study published in the *New England Journal of Medicine* in 2006 stated, "health insurance status was largely unrelated to the quality of health care." [71]

Barack Obama has preyed for too long on the hearts and minds of Americans who may be misinformed about the state of health care and health insurance in the United States. He claims to represent a change in American politics today yet he is willing to provide dishonest information to his audience in a bid to sway public opinion and win an election.

## FREE MARKET SOLUTIONS LEAD TO LOWER COST & BETTER CARE

> Third, we will reduce the cost of our health care by improving the quality of our health care. Much like the hospital report cards we passed in Illinois, my health care proposal will ask hospitals and providers to collect, track, and publicly report measures of health care quality... [72]

With his limited amount of political experience, Barack Obama believes that more government control will improve the cost and quality of health care. The exact opposite is true. Allowing businesses in the health care sector to innovate allows for more choices for customers and sets the stage for future success in the industry.

Within the past few years, clinics have begun to spring up all throughout the country to meet the rising demand of effective, low cost health care. Dubbed, "convenient clinics," they are found in pharmacies or Wal-marts and offer an alternative to a doctor's office or a hospital. They provide basic health care services at a fraction of the time and price and are mostly staffed by certified registered nurses. They treat common ailments such as colds, sore throats and ear infections. They also administer basic physicals exams, immunizations, and yearly checkups.

These clinics deliver something that many hospitals cannot-- cheap, effective and timely health care. There are no appointments needed and most clinics are open seven days a week. Customers are able to see exactly what they pay for by examining a list of prices displayed at the clinic. Some services cost under $20 and many insurance plans, including Medicare, will pick up the tab.

Barack Obama wants to create more government bureaucracy by having providers initiate plans to record and track health care quality in the United States. Adhering to free-market principles however would allow people to receive care quickly, and at a fraction of the cost.

Several medical professionals support convenient clinics. Rather than oppose the clinics, The American Academy of Family Physicians published a list of basic standards they believed should be followed. Representing more than 90,000 family practitioners, the AAFP realized these clinics help people receive quality health care at a reduced cost. The Clinics responded by accepting the standards and in many cases even required their employers to adhere to more rigorous benchmarks. [73]

It is unfortunate that Barack Obama refuses to acknowledge advancements in the medical community that are allowing private companies to play a role in the health and wellness of the American people. He continues to push for a government monopoly on health care that will hurt those people with the most immediate needs. His far left agenda must not be allowed to corrupt the enduring spirit of the American political system tradition.

## WILL SWITCHING TO ELECTRONIC RECORDS SAVE LIVES?

> Fourth, we will reduce waste and inefficiency by moving from a 20th century health care industry based on pen and paper to a 21st century industry based on the latest information technology. By moving to electronic medical records, we can give doctors and nurses easy access to all the necessary information about their patients... This will reduce deadly medical errors... and save billions and billions of dollars in the process.[74]

The idea of shifting from paper records to electronic records is not a new concept. The idea has been implemented by countless clinics and hospitals, and numerous politicians encourage the practice. From a business perspective, it could limit administrative costs, thereby lowering the overall cost of operating hospitals. The problem arises from Obama's pledge to have government mandate the program.

Will changing the way records are kept really save billions of dollars as Obama suggests? More importantly, will it really save lives? The evidence seems to suggest that Barack Obama's quick fix solution has some gaping holes. According to a study published in the July 9th edition of the *Archives of Internal Medicine*, records being kept electronically had little impact on the overall quality of care when it came to walk-in doctor visits. [75] "In clinic visits in which doctors did use and didn't use electronic health records, we didn't find clear evidence that EHR [Electronic Health Record] use was associated with better quality," said study lead author Dr. Jeffrey Linder. [76]

Obama's claim that electronic records will save lives by reducing medical errors would be a welcome addition to the health care industry, if it were true. However can anything Barack Obama says be taken at face value? Despite what medium the records are kept, doctors need to prescribe the correct medication, monitor past illnesses and spell their patients' names correctly. Mistakes can be made just as easily with pen and paper as they can with a keyboard. "There's nothing magical about electronic health records," says Linder. "You need to have tools in place that take advantage of technology to show improvements in quality. You need to do additional work instead of just turning on the computer." [77]

To test the effectiveness of electronic health records, Linder and his staff evaluated visits to physicians' offices that only required outpatient care. They then cross-referenced the visits against 17 factors they determined were most important to the quality of the care. Overall, the study determined that electronic health records were not directly associated with a better quality of care. In some cases, such as the prescription of statins to patients with high cholesterol, the study found that electronic health records actually provided a lower quality of care. [78]

> Finally, we will break the stranglehold that a few big drug
> and insurance companies have on the health care market.
> They'll sell the same exact drugs here in America for double
> the price of what they charge in Europe and Canada… We
> don't have to stand for that anymore. Under my plan, we
> will make generic drugs more available to consumers and
> we will tell the drug companies that their days of forcing
> affordable prescription drugs out of the market are over.[79]

It is curious that those on the left rarely criticize businessmen like George
Soros or Ted Turner for turning a profit and raking in millions of dollars
each year. So why is Barack Obama so focused on private companies in
the health care industry? Obama believes that nationalizing the health
care system will fix the problem of "greedy" corporations that don't
provide the best care to their patients. Like the story of Shirley Healey,
the question we must ask ourselves is: If individuals are receiving care
and being treated properly, does it really matter if someone else is making
a profit? More so, will government involvement really cause health
care to be less expensive? "This is the country of medical innovation,"
says Dr. David Gretzer. "This is where people come when they need
treatment. Literally we're surrounded by medical miracles." [80]

Private companies are responsible for the medical innovations we see
today. The government gives us the Post Office and the Department of
Motor Vehicles while the private sector gives us flat screen televisions
and digital cameras. Private industry generates competition between
companies. This leads to better quality products and a reduced cost for
consumers. When it comes to the medical field, private industry leads
to new and effective treatments and medicines. With no competition,
government control over health care would lead to higher prices and
a massive decline in quality. Hospitals in places like Great Britain
are being forced to cut services in order to cut costs. Controlled by
the National Health Service, some hospitals have resorted to asking
patients to bring drugs in from home, or removing every third light bulb
from hallways and corridors. [81] With a budget deficit of almost $12
million, one government-controlled hospital even encouraged staff to

save money on laundry costs by flipping over dirty bed sheets between patients instead of washing them.[82]

Government control limits the choices people have when looking for care and it prevents patients from receiving the best care possible. By allowing private businesses to administer prices, we produce the best available products and the best quality care. "Drug companies looking to make money invest in things that improve our quality of life and save lives," says 20/20 host John Stossel.[83] It is *because* drug companies are looking to make a profit that they continue to find ways to create and perfect new medications. They know they must remain one step ahead of the competition if they wish to stay in business. The drug company Pfizer alone produces over 150 types of medications. From Accupril to Celebrex; from Lipitor to Viagra; from Xanax to Zoloft; these medications have saved lives and provided a better quality of life for millions of Americans.[84]

## MEDICARE: GREAT FAILURE OF THE GREAT SOCIETY

> Half a century ago, America found itself in the midst
> of another health care crisis... And finally, after years of
> advocacy and negotiation and plenty of setbacks, President
> Lyndon Johnson signed the Medicare bill into law on July
> 30th of 1965. And as he stood with [Harry] Truman by
> his side and signed what would become one of the most
> successful government programs in history President
> Johnson looked out at the crowd and said, "History shapes
> men, but it is a necessary faith of leadership that men can
> help shape history.[85]

Perhaps no statement made by Barack Obama sums up his inability to be President more than the above. Should any politician who honestly refers to Medicare as a success truly be taken seriously? Medicare has done substantial and perhaps irreparable damage to the health care system. Medicare increased costs, limited patient choices, and provided a poorer quality of care than what was previously available. And yet within Barack Obama's twisted logic is an ironic truth to the statement. Referring to Medicare as one of the most successful government programs in history is tantamount to calling Ted Bundy one of the least dangerous serial killers in history. Though the statement may not be false in and of itself, it represents a massive break from conventional wisdom. Like so many government programs born out of the social welfare movement, Medicare has proven itself to be a complete and utter failure.

## EXPOSING BARACK OBAMA'S SOCIALIST AGENDA

> The time has come for affordable, universal health care in America. And I look forward to working with all of you to meet this challenge in the weeks and months to come. Thank you.[86]

The time has indeed come, though not for the costly and expensive health care that Barack Obama desires. The American people must stand firm and reject the lies and false logic Obama has tried to spoon-feed them. As he has made his way from the Illinois State Senate to his party's Presidential nomination, Barack Obama has made it clear that his ultimate goal is to put the United States on a path to socialism. We must discard the hollow words of Obama's empty promises and see that this grossly under-qualified candidate is exposed for what he really is. Only when we adhere to the founding principles of our government and follow true free market solutions, will the American people have access to health care that is affordable, dependable, and above all, effective.

32    "Remarks of Senator Barack Obama," *New York Times*, http://www.ny-times.com/2007/05/29/us/politics/28text-obama.html?pagewanted=1&r=3&adxnnl=1&adxnnlx=1214852159-0BeBq1hXdAdSNF6vB2T/HQ (29 May 2007).

33    "U.S. Health Care Politics," *CBS News/New York Times Poll*, http://www.cbsnews.com/htdocs/CBSNews_polls/health_care.pdf (1 March 2007).

34    "U.S. Health Care Politics," *CBS News/New York Times Poll*, http://www.cbsnews.com/htdocs/CBSNews_polls/health_care.pdf (1 March 2007).

35    "Remarks of Senator Barack Obama," *New York Times*, http://www.ny-times.com/2007/05/29/us/politics/28text-obama.html?pagewanted=1&r=3&adxnnl=1&adxnnlx=1214852159-0BeBq1hXdAdSNF6vB2T/HQ (29 May 2007).

36    Scott Helman, "In Illinois, Obama dealt with lobbyists," *Boston Globe*," http://www.boston.com/news/nation/articles/2007/09/23/in_illinois_obama_dealt_with_lobbyists/ (23 September, 2007).

37    Scott Helman, "In Illinois, Obama dealt with lobbyists," *Boston Globe*," http://www.boston.com/news/nation/articles/2007/09/23/in_illinois_obama_dealt_with_lobbyists/ (23 September, 2007).

38    "Remarks of Senator Barack Obama," *New York Times*, http://www.ny-times.com/2007/05/29/us/politics/28text-obama.html?pagewanted=1&r=3&adxnnl=1&adxnnlx=1214852159-0BeBq1hXdAdSNF6vB2T/HQ (29 May 2007).

39    "Employer Health Benefits 2007 Annual Survey," *The Kaiser Family Foundation and Health Research and Educational Trust*, http://www.kff.org/insurance/7672/upload/76723.pdf

40    "Remarks of Senator Barack Obama," *New York Times*, http://www.nytimes.com/2007/05/29/us/politics/28textobama.html?_r=4&adxnnl=1&pagewanted=2&adxnnlx=1215976310-UHcC6Thv/EIIY/lnYkmOfg (29 May 2007).

41    John Stossel, "Sick in America," *20/20*, (14 September 2007).

42    John Stossel, "Sick in America," *20/20*, (14 September 2007).

43  "Remarks of Senator Barack Obama," *New York Times*, http://www.
    nytimes.com/2007/05/29/us/politics/28text-obama.html?_r=4&adxnnl=
    1&pagewanted=2&adxnnlx=1215976310-UHcC6Thv/EIIY/lnYkmOfg
    (29 May 2007).

44  John, Stossel, *Give Me a Break* (Harper Collins: New York, 2004), p. 44.

45  "Remarks of Senator Barack Obama," *New York Times*, http://www.
    nytimes.com/2007/05/29/us/politics/28text-obama.html?_r=4&adxnnl=
    1&pagewanted=2&adxnnlx=1215976310-UHcC6Thv/EIIY/lnYkmOfg
    (29 May 2007).

46  William Faloon, "FDA's Lethal Impediment," *Life Extension Magazine*,
    http://www.lef.org/magazine/mag2003/aug2003_awsi_01.html.

47  "Remarks of Senator Barack Obama," *New York Times*, http://www.
    nytimes.com/2007/05/29/us/politics/28text-obama.html?_r=4&adxnnl=
    1&pagewanted=2&adxnnlx=1215976310-UHcC6Thv/EIIY/lnYkmOfg
    (29 May 2007)

48  "Barack H. Obama U.S. Individual Income Tax Return," *Internal
    Revenue Service*, http://msnbcmedia.msn.com/i/msnbc/sections/tvnews/
    nightly%20news/_tab%20boxes/obama_tax_return.pdf.

49  "Remarks of Senator Barack Obama," *New York Times*, http://www.ny-
    times.com/2007/05/29/us/politics/28text-obama.html?pagewanted=3&_
    r=4&adxnnlx=1215976310-UHcC6Thv/EIIY/lnYkmOfg (29 May
    2007).

50  "Bill Status of HB2268," *Illinois General Assembly*, http://www.ilga.gov/
    legislation/BillStatus.asp?DocNum=2268&GAID=3&DocTypeID=HB&
    LegId=3499&SessionID=3&GA=93.

51  "Bill Status of HB2268," *Illinois General Assembly*, http://www.ilga.gov/
    legislation/BillStatus.asp?DocNum=2268&GAID=3&DocTypeID=HB&
    LegId=3499&SessionID=3&GA=93.

52  "Remarks of Senator Barack Obama," *New York Times*, http://www.ny-
    times.com/2007/05/29/us/politics/28text-obama.html?pagewanted=3&_
    r=4&adxnnlx=1215976310-UHcC6Thv/EIIY/lnYkmOfg (29 May
    2007).

53   "Paying a Premium: The Added Cost of Care for the Uninsured," *Families USA*, http://www.familiesusa.org/assets/pdfs/Paying_a_Premium731e.pdf.

54   "Paying a Premium: The Added Cost of Care for the Uninsured," *Families USA*, http://www.familiesusa.org/assets/pdfs/Paying_a_Premium731e.pdf.

55   "Paying a Premium: The Added Cost of Care for the Uninsured," *Families USA*, http://www.familiesusa.org/assets/pdfs/Paying_a_Premium731e.pdf.

56   "Remarks of Senator Barack Obama," *New York Times*, http://www.nytimes.com/2007/05/29/us/politics/28text-obama.html?pagewanted=3&_r=4&adxnnlx=1215976310-UHcC6Thv/EIIY/lnYkmOfg (29 May 2007).

57   Cheryl Hill Lee, Bernadette D. Proctor, Carmen DeNavas-Walt, "Income, Poverty, and Health Insurance Coverage in the United States: 2005," *U.S. Census Bureau*, http://www.census.gov/prod/2006pubs/p60-231.pdf (August 2006).

58   Cheryl Hill Lee, Bernadette D. Proctor, Carmen DeNavas-Walt, "Income, Poverty, and Health Insurance Coverage in the United States: 2005," *U.S. Census Bureau*, http://www.census.gov/prod/2006pubs/p60-231.pdf (August 2006).

59   Cheryl Hill Lee, Bernadette D. Proctor, Carmen DeNavas-Walt, "Income, Poverty, and Health Insurance Coverage in the United States: 2005," *U.S. Census Bureau*, http://www.census.gov/prod/2006pubs/p60-231.pdf (August 2006).

60   Julia A. Seymour, "Health Care Lie: '47 Million Uninsured Americans'," *Business and Media Institute*, http://www.freemarketproject.org/articles/2007/20070718153509.aspx (18 July 2007).

61   Julia A. Seymour, "Health Care Lie: '47 Million Uninsured Americans'," *Business and Media Institute*, http://www.freemarketproject.org/articles/2007/20070718153509.aspx (18 July 2007).

62   Julia A. Seymour, "Health Care Lie: '47 Million Uninsured Americans'," *Business and Media Institute*, *http://www.freemarketproject.org/articles/2007/20070718153509.aspx* (18 July 2007).

63  "Remarks of Senator Barack Obama," *New York Times,* http://www.ny-times.com/2007/05/29/us/politics/28text-obama.html?pagewanted=3&_r=4&adxnnlx=1215976310-UHcC6Thv/EIIY/lnYkmOfg (29 May 2007).

64  Michael D. Tanner, "Moore's Sick Rx," *CATO Institute,* http://www.cato.org/pub_display.php?pub_id=8271.

65  Giles Whittell, "Michael, keep away. The NHS is a rip-off," *Times Online,* http://www.timesonline.co.uk/tol/comment/columnists/article2039584.ece (7 July 2007).

66  "Remarks of Senator Barack Obama," *New York Times,* http://www.ny-times.com/2007/05/29/us/politics/28text-obama.html?pagewanted=3&_r=4&adxnnlx=1215976310-UHcC6Thv/EIIY/lnYkmOfg (29 May 2007).

67  John Stossel, "Sick in America," *20/20,* (14 September 2007).

68  "Remarks of Senator Barack Obama," *New York Times,* http://www.ny-times.com/2007/05/29/us/politics/28text-obama.html?pagewanted=3&_r=4&adxnnlx=1215976310-UHcC6Thv/EIIY/lnYkmOfg (29 May 2007).

69  Michael Cannon, Michael Tanner, "Universal healthcare's dirty little secrets," *Los Angeles Times,* http://www.latimes.com/news/opinion/la-oe-tanner5apr05,0,2227144.story?coll=la-opinion-rightrail (5 April 2007).

70  Michael Cannon, Michael Tanner, "Universal healthcare's dirty little secrets," *Los Angeles Times,* http://www.latimes.com/news/opinion/la-oe-tanner5apr05,0,2227144.story?coll=la-opinion-rightrail (5 April 2007).

71  Michael Cannon, Michael Tanner, "Universal healthcare's dirty little secrets," *Los Angeles Times,* http://www.latimes.com/news/opinion/la-oe-tanner5apr05,0,2227144.story?coll=la-opinion-rightrail (5 April 2007).

72  "Remarks of Senator Barack Obama," *New York Times,* http://www.ny-times.com/2007/05/29/us/politics/28text-obama.html?pagewanted=4&_r=4&adxnnlx=1215976310-UHcC6Thv/EIIY/lnYkmOfg (29 May 2007).

73  Web Golinkin, "Health Care When You Want It," *Wall Street Journal,* (2 August 2007).

74   "Remarks of Senator Barack Obama," *New York Times,* http://www.ny-times.com/2007/05/29/us/politics/28text-obama.html?pagewanted=4&_r=4&adxnnlx=1215976310-UHcC6Thv/EIIY/lnYkmOfg (29 May 2007).

75   David W. Bates, Jeffrey A. Linder, Blackford Middleton, Randall S. Stafford, "Electronic Health Record Use and the Quality of Ambulatory Care in the United States," *Archives of Internal Medicine,* http://archinte.ama-assn.org/cgi/content/abstract/167/13/1400.

76   Amanda Gardner, "Electronic Records Don't Always Improve Care," *Washington Post,* http://www.washingtonpost.com/wp-dyn/content/article/2007/07/10/AR2007071000487.html (10 July 2007).

77   Amanda Gardner, "Electronic Records Don't Always Improve Care," *Washington Post,* http://www.washingtonpost.com/wp-dyn/content/article/2007/07/10/AR2007071000487.html (10 July 2007).

78   David W. Bates, Jeffrey A. Linder, Blackford Middleton, Randall S. Stafford, "Electronic Health Record Use and the Quality of Ambulatory Care in the United States," *Archives of Internal Medicine,* http://archinte.ama-assn.org/cgi/content/abstract/167/13/1400.

79   "Remarks of Senator Barack Obama," *New York Times,* http://www.ny-times.com/2007/05/29/us/politics/28text-obama.html?pagewanted=4&_r=4&adxnnlx=1215976310-UHcC6Thv/EIIY/lnYkmOfg (29 May 2007).

80   John Stossel, "Sick in America," *20/20,* (14 September 2007).

81   Daniel Martin, "Hard-up hospital orders staff: Don't wash sheets – turn them over," *Mail Online,* http://www.dailymail.co.uk/health/article-448395/Hard-hospital-orders-staff-Dont-wash-sheets--turn-over.html (13 April 2007).

82   Daniel Martin, "Hard-up hospital orders staff: Don't wash sheets – turn them over," *Mail Online,* http://www.dailymail.co.uk/health/article-448395/Hard-hospital-orders-staff-Dont-wash-sheets--turn-over.html (13 April 2007).

83   John Stossel, "Sick in America," *20/20,* (14 September 2007).

84   "Products," *Pfizer Pharmaceuticals,* http://www.pfizer.com/products/.

[85] "Remarks of Senator Barack Obama," *New York Times,* http://www.nytimes.com/2007/05/29/us/politics/28text-obama.html?pagewanted=5&_r=4&adxnnlx=1215976310-UHcC6Thv/EIIY/lnYkmOfg (29 May 2007).

[86] "Remarks of Senator Barack Obama," *New York Times,* http://www.nytimes.com/2007/05/29/us/politics/28text-obama.html?pagewanted=5&_r=4&adxnnlx=1215976310-UHcC6Thv/EIIY/lnYkmOfg (29 May 2007).

# CHAPTER 4

## CITIZENS OF THE REPUBLIC:
## BARACK OBAMA ON IMMIGRATION AND CULTURE

"You can't create experience. You must undergo it."

- Albert Camus, French Author

Barack Obama served eight years in the Illinois State Senate and fewer than four in the United States Senate. His limited experience immediately calls into question his ability to serve as the most powerful man in the world. An even greater uncertainty than his inexperience, however, is his attitude toward the law he must swear to uphold upon entering office. Along with the burden of the Presidency comes the responsibility of serving one's citizens with honor. A President must respect the history, culture, and law of the great men who came before him.

Obama has charmed his way to a Presidential nomination using his oratory skills and personal charisma. But those who look closer see the illusion fade, and find a young man without regard for history or Constitutional tradition. They find a man bent on transforming the United States into a radical left shell of what it once stood for, and what it could stand for again.

Barack Obama betrayed U.S. law in favor of naïvely embracing the millions of illegal immigrants flocking across the United States border.

He expressed no disdain or remorse as the values of an American culture and a unifying language began to fade away. He issued no call to preserve that for which our forefathers fought and died.

Throughout our proud history, many United States Presidents have remained at their post, fanning the flame of the American spirit. These men defended the American dream and kept American culture alive. Today, the citizens of this republic stand ready to protect their nation and their way of life from those who would manipulate and usurp such freedom.

Those who wish to protect the American dream of liberty must be ever vigilant. They must be men of words backed up by action, thoughtful and well informed, following in the footsteps of our forefathers and learning from their experiences. These men stood ready to protect the American dream, and American civilization. Barack Obama is not one of these men.

***

"A melting pot, yes. A tower of Babel, no."

- Saul Bellow, Canadian-born American Author

## EDUCATION FOR ILLEGAL IMMIGRANTS

By serving eight years in the Illinois State Senate and sponsoring more than 800 bills, one would think there would be much evidence regarding Barack Obama's stance on immigration, both legal and illegal. According to a *New York Times* article in July of 2007 however, this is not the case. Of the 823 bills Obama proposed during his time in the state senate only one was identified by the *Times* as dealing directly with "immigration;" a 2003 proposal to create an office of immigrant assistance to provide education and outreach services to the immigrant community. Digging deeper through the archives of the Illinois State Senate, we find that in addition to the bill referenced by the paper,

70

there were a number of other bills sponsored by Obama relating to immigration and culture.

While lobbying for President in December of 2007 the Obama campaign wrote to its supporters, "As an Illinois State Senator and a United States Senator, I have worked hard to improve our nation's immigration laws. For example, I strongly supported legislation before the Illinois State Senate that would have helped honest and hard-working immigrant students attend college by providing them with government loans to pay for tuition." [87]

The legislation he was most likely referring to was a bill proposed to the Illinois State Senate almost five years to the day prior; an early Christmas gift to the tax payers of Illinois. On December 23, 2002 State Representative Edward J. Acavedo filed HB0060 within the Illinois General Assembly. This bill allowed illegal immigrants and their children to qualify for in-state tuition at public universities throughout the state, at taxpayer expense. Obama became a co-sponsor to the bill on April 10, 2003 as the bill was being pushed through the legislature.

Four stipulations were established to determine residency in the state of Illinois and therefore eligibility for in-state tuition. If the resident was not an American citizen however, only one stipulation applied; a promise to attempt to become a U.S. citizen as soon as possible. The bill stated:

> In the case of an individual who is not a citizen or a
> permanent resident of the United States, the individual
> provides the University with an affidavit stating that the
> individual will file an application to become a permanent
> resident of the United States at the earliest opportunity the
> individual is eligible to do so. [88]

According to the 2008 Scholarship Handbook put out by College Board, the cost of public education at four year colleges continues to increase, rising more than 6.5% from 2007 to 2008 and currently standing at an average of $6,185 a year per student. There are an estimated 400,000 illegal aliens living in the state of Illinois along. [89]

The effects of the bill signed into law in 2003 were not confined only to colleges. The Federation for American Immigration Reform estimates that in 2004, Obama's final year in the state senate, Illinois taxpayers spent more than two billion dollars on public education for illegal immigrants and their children. [90] In his zeal to aid "hard working immigrant students," Barack Obama threw hard working American citizens (and taxpayers) under the bus and left them to deal with any problems that might arise.

## UNITE IN WORDS, DIVIDE IN ACTION

On January 9, 2003, Barack Obama filed a bill designed to amend the Illinois Freedom of Information Act. The bill's main focus was seemingly to increase the personal privacy of citizens within the state. However the bill did not stop there. Digging deeper allows one to see the additional components Obama inserted into the text.

The bill, SB0030 would also require the Department of State Police to provide training to its officers concerning sensitivity toward, "racial and ethnic differences." In addition to altering the state Freedom of Information Act, the bill sought to amend the Department of State Police Law of the Civil Administrative Code of Illinois, the Illinois Police Training Act, the State Mandates Act, and the Illinois Vehicle Code. Section 2605-85 of the bill stated:

> The department shall provide training and continuing
> education to state police officers concerning cultural
> diversity, including sensitivity toward racial and ethnic
> differences. This training and continuing education shall
> include, but not be limited to, an emphasis on the fact that
> the primary purpose of enforcement of the Illinois Vehicle
> Code is safety and equal and uniform enforcement under
> the law. [91]

The bill also provided for a four-year study based on information recorded from traffic stops or warning citations by state and local law enforcement. It is important that when criticizing Barack Obama for his far left agenda that he be given the same courtesy as any politician from the middle or the right. Taxes are levied for specified reasons after all, and the government does provide certain services to its people with that revenue. With the bill also stating that the primary purpose of enforcement of the Illinois Vehicle Code is "safety" and "equal and uniform enforcement under the law," is Obama's claim valid? Are the proper steps taken to ensure all races are being given equal treatment? Or do additional steps need to be taken to ensure traffic safety is improved in regards to the Motor Vehicle Code?

By examining the rate of motor vehicle theft in the years before and after Barack Obama's bill took effect, we see just the opposite took place. According to the Illinois State Police's Uniform Crime Report, in 2002 the rate of motor vehicle theft fell by 8% across the state. This was the greatest drop in motor vehicle theft since Illinois began collecting additional crime statistics in 1996 as mandated by state statute in accordance with the federal government.

Upon the passage of Obama's bill designed to focus more police efforts on racial sensitivity, the drop in motor vehicle crime actually slowed. In actuality, since the bill's passage in 2003, decline slowed down considerably. The highest percentage drop in motor vehicle theft came in 2002, the year before Obama proposed the bill.

### Year% Drop in Motor Vehicle Theft

| Year | % Drop |
|------|--------|
| 2001-2002 | 8.0% |
| 2002-2003 | 7.3% |
| 2003-2004 | 3.6% |
| 2004-2005 | 3.0% [92] |

Barack Obama's bill did nothing to improve motor vehicle safety. Obama used taxpayer dollars to fund a program that was unnecessary and actually led to a reduction in the drop of crime rates.

# ILLEGALS - 1
# CITIZENS - 0

Perhaps no aspect of the debate on illegal immigration has so incensed American citizens more than the blatant disregard for the law shown by millions. This disregard is not confined only to illegal immigrants however. As illegal immigrants march through the streets and demand government services, it is allies and politicians on the far left whom have proven their willingness to obey.

A clear example of this was a bill introduced by Barack Obama in February of 2003. That month Obama co-sponsored SB0679, a bill effectively taking rights away from employers and transferring them to illegal immigrants. The most egregious article of the bill was section 2-102, which made it illegal for an employer to refuse employment based upon a worker's citizenship status. The section stated:

> It is a civil rights violation... For any employer to refuse to hire... on the basis of unlawful discrimination or citizenship status. [93]

Employers and small business owners were legally prevented from denying a job to an applicant solely based on whether or not he was an illegal immigrant. While most people would agree this quality alone is enough to disqualify someone for a job, Obama instead helped pass legislation that would allow more illegal immigrants to take jobs away from American citizens.

## REACHING OUT... TO PICK YOUR POCKET...

As stated previously, a July 2007 article by the *New York Times* listed only one bill sponsored by Barack Obama dealing directly with the topic of immigration. SB0680 is that such bill. Co-sponsored by Obama and filed on February 19 of that same year the bill amended the Attorney General Act to create an "Office of

Immigrant Assistance" within the Office of the Attorney General. The bill states:

> These immigrants often require assistance in order to obtain the government services to which they are entitled under the law. [94]

The sense of entitlement promoted by Barack Obama and his far left agenda is perhaps nowhere better personified than in the pages of this bill. Through generations of legal immigration to the United States, millions of people are the descendents of those who came to this country searching for a better life. Whether they are their children, grandchildren, great grandchildren or beyond, they share a common history and a common unifying factor; that their ancestors came to this nation desiring to be Americans. According to Barack Obama however, immigrants are now "entitled" to government services at taxpayer expense. The bill continues:

> Within the Office of the Attorney General, there shall be established an Immigrant Assistance Program, which shall be charged with the responsibility of assessing the needs of the State's immigrant community with regard to access to government and other services. [95]

One wonders exactly what "education and outreach services" consist of? The bill was conveniently silent on this topic. However a fiscal note added by the Office of the Attorney General gave some insight on what the expected cost would be.

> The estimated annual cost would be $300,000. This would include salary and benefits for 2 new full-time AAGs and 1.5 support staff, plus their related operating costs [96]

Obama has established that he is willing to divert hard earned money from American citizens and use it to give illegal aliens a number of free government services.

## Embracing Change, Avoiding Controversy

Appearing unexpectedly on the national political scene, Barack Obama has built himself up as the candidate separate from the typical politicians of the day. He has campaigned as one with the ability to separate himself from infighting, stand above bitter rivalries, and emerge distinct from leaders of the past. But is he really any different at all?

As far back as 1999 we see examples of Obama's similarity to other politicians of the day. In that year, Obama stood in the middle of a difficult vote—whether or not juveniles in the criminal justice system could be tried as adults. On one hand, Obama risked sabotaging his "tough on crime" image. On the other, he risked upsetting those in the black community; the demographic expected to be most affected by the decision. In the end Obama decided to stand on neither side of the aisle and voted "present," effectively abstaining from the vote.

Barack Obama was not the first politician to abstain from a controversial vote, nor will he be the last. Yet much like his unwillingness to be forthright with his records from the Illinois State Senate, we see that with the exception of his far left agenda, Obama is no different from other politicians of our time. The above was not an isolated incident. During his term in the state senate, Obama voted "present" nearly 130 times, abstaining from votes instead of taking a stand on their policy or their procedure. [97]

As Barack Obama was elected to the United States Senate in 2004, the focus of his far left agenda shifted. No longer would only the state of Illinois be privy to his bills, speeches, and resolutions. Now the entire United States would be subject to his ideology as he made Washington DC his home and the chambers of the United States Senate his bully pulpit.

> "The gift of a common tongue is a priceless inheritance and
> it may well someday become the foundation of a common
> citizenship."

> - Winston Churchill, British Statesman

## MEXICO FIRST, GUATEMALA SECOND, AMERICA IF THERE'S TIME

Taking office in January of 2005, Obama brought with him an aura of prestige to the steps of the United States Senate. Coming off the media hype surrounding his speech at the Democratic National Convention that past summer, Obama was featured on the cover of *Newsweek* Magazine's year end review alongside the tagline, "Seeing Purple: A Rising Star Who Wants to Get Beyond Blue vs. Red." [98] While Obama would continue to ride the favorable press all the way to the Democratic National Convention in 2008, it would soon become clear the man behind the curtain was neither great nor powerful. The apparent aura of prestige was nothing more than a smokescreen put in place to allow Barack Obama to push his radically left agenda even further.

In May of that year, the senate began what would become the first of three yearly debates concerning illegal immigration and the protection of our nation's borders. On May 12, 2005 legislation was introduced onto the floor of the United States Senate as S. 1033, better known as the Secure America and Orderly Immigration Act. Barack Obama added his name to the legislation and officially designated himself as a co-sponsor later in the year.

The bill dealt with guest worker programs and border enforcement as well as offering a path to citizenship for illegal aliens already within the United States. Its proponents attempted to brush off the ensuing cries of "amnesty," claiming that immigrants here illegally would have to pay financial restitution and be privy to other regulations. [99] Unfortunately that mindset has come to represent much of the pro-illegal immigrant movement within our nation. No longer do politicians such as Barack

77

Obama believe in the system of justice we have established. Instead of a nation of law the United States is seen as a nation of convenience.

In addition to the clauses for amnesty, perhaps the most curious aspect of the bill was additional text inserted to protect the border. The border in question is not the United States border, seeing how numerous other pages of the bill stated procedure and enforcement strategies regarding the American boundaries. Instead one inexplicable aspect of the bill was the inclusion of a plan to protect the southern border, not of the United States, but of Mexico. Title I, Subtitle C, Section 133 of the bill discussed at length the responsibility of the United States to maintain and enforce law within Mexico and numerous Central American countries. It stated:

> The Secretary of State, in coordination with the Secretary of Homeland Security… shall establish a program to— assess the specific needs of the governments of Central American countries in maintaining the security of the borders of such countries. [100]

Perhaps even more upsetting was a section of the bill that outlined steps the US would take to implement the border security plan. Once again the plan did not focus on defending our nation by patrolling the border between Mexico and the United States, but by patrolling the border between Mexico and Guatemala. The bill stated:

> The Secretary of State, in consultation with the Secretary of Homeland Security, the Government of Mexico and appropriate officials of the Governments of Guatemala, Belize, and neighboring contiguous countries, shall establish a program to provide needed equipment, technical assistance, and vehicles to manage, regulate, and patrol the international border between Mexico and Guatemala and between Mexico and Belize.[101]

The Secure America and Orderly Immigration Act of 2005 gained national attention by attracting some members of both parties. Along with Republicans weak on the defense of immigration and culture, the bill attracted the likes of far left senators such as Ted Kennedy, Ken Salazar, John Kerry, and of course Barack Obama. If successful, the bill could have rewarded millions of illegal aliens with amnesty. Thankfully the legislation made it no further than its referral to the Judiciary Committee.

## A SECOND ATTEMPT AT AMNESTY

Almost a year to the day later, a second bill was brought to the floor of the U.S. Senate dealing with immigration and border security within the United States. Known as the Comprehensive Immigration Reform Act of 2006, S. 2611 sought to pick up the pieces from the broken immigration act of 2005. The bill would bring passionate responses from both sides of the floor, with 150 separate amendments proposed to the bill before the end of debate. [102]

One month prior; as the bill made its way through the bureaucracy and paper work necessary to reach the Senate floor, Barack Obama addressed his fellow legislators. On April 3rd, Obama stated, "The American people are a welcoming and generous people. But those who enter our country illegally, and those who employ them, disrespect the rule of law... We simply cannot allow people to pour into the United States undetected, undocumented, and unchecked. Americans are right to demand better border security and better enforcement of the immigration laws." [103]

Had Barack Obama softened his previous hard left stance? Had he come to see the importance of the law and the defense of American culture and security? Unfortunately he had not. Once again arguing for a barter of amnesty for financial penalty, Obama's speech took a sharp turn to the left. He continued,

...But in exchange for accepting those penalties, we
must allow undocumented immigrants to come out of
the shadows and step on a path toward full participation
in our society. In fact, I will not support any bill that
does not provide this earned path to citizenship for the
undocumented population...[104]

Barack Obama's words would represent a major break within the chambers of the Senate and throughout the nation. Over the next few weeks, marches and rallies were organized in dozens of cities across the country. While proponents of illegal immigration were quick to point out the lack of violence at most of these protests, they rarely spoke of the overwhelming number of Mexican and Central American flags brought by the crowds. Students from one high school in Montebello, California even made national headlines when they took down an American flag from the courtyard flagpole and positioned the Mexican flag in its place. They then turned the American flag upside down, (a term commonly used to signal distress,) and raised both symbols, with the Mexican flag flying above that of the stars and stripes.[105]

The Comprehensive Immigration Reform Act was introduced in early April and would see more than six weeks of discussion and debate on the senate floor as well as in conference rooms and committee meetings. Numerous amendments were proposed to the legislation, and it is from these amendments we are able to gain a better understanding of the agenda and ideology of Barack Obama.

On May 18, Senator James Inhofe of Oklahoma proposed Amendment 4064. The text of the amendment was short and sweet with its purpose fairly self-explanatory. The amendment's byline of purpose read:

To amend title 4 United States Code, to declare English as
the national language of the United States and to promote
the patriotic integration of prospective US citizens. [106]

Those puzzled why an amendment like this is necessary should note the current state of affairs regarding language in the United States. Despite valiant attempts by organizations such as US-English and other educational foundations, the English tongue is not the official language of the United States. [107] America officially has no national language at all and according to Barack Obama that is how it should remain. Obama voted against the amendment, further widening the divide between himself and the American citizens he supposedly represents. Despite Obama's vote however, the amendment passed. This was a testament to those in the Senate standing up for the American way of life.

On that very same day Obama's fellow Senator (and former Presidential challenger) Hillary Clinton proposed an amendment dealing with the federal government's ever-increasing role in providing education and health care to illegal aliens. Known as the "State Criminal Alien Assistance Program" Amendment, S. 4072 established a grant program in which state and local government could apply to. The bill stated that federal tax dollars would be used:

> ...for the cost of providing health care and educational
> services to noncitizens...[108]

Apparently someone failed to mention to Mr. Obama that the enforcement of law is one of the primary responsibilities of the federal government. Obama instead focused on providing services to those here illegally and immediately signed on as a co-sponsor of the bill. The bill was brought to the floor and received a vote within a matter of hours, where it failed to pass.

Unlike a similar bill proposed in the House of Representatives, the Senate's Comprehensive Immigration Reform Act of 2006 opened up a path to citizenship for approximately 10 million illegal immigrants. Much like the legislation of the previous year, supporters of the bill claimed it held lawbreakers accountable by making them pass a background check and pay specified back taxes. [109] But the bill was almost a carbon copy of

2005's legislation. Offering amnesty to millions of illegal aliens, the bill undermined the very essence of the American justice system and granted a reprieve to millions of people who blatantly disregarded the values of the nation and further contributed to a breakdown in the rule of law.

Aiding in this breakdown was Barack Obama, who voted for the bill and contributed to its passage on May 25, 2006. [110] Ironically it was only after the vote that the bureaucratic paperwork assembly line, better known as the United States Federal Government, actually helped the citizens of our republic defend the rule of law within our borders. Despite passage of the bill, it failed it committee and never became law. The end of the 109th Congress in January of 2007 marked the termination of the bill. The stage was set for round three.

## THE RULE OF LAW UNDER ATTACK

Another year would pass before the Senate brought yet another attempt at "Immigration Reform" with S. 1348; better known as the Comprehensive Immigration Reform Act of 2007. Once again proposed in the month of May, the bill was introduced by Harry Reid, Democratic Senator from Nevada. Though the bill itself never came to a vote, one amendment in particular stands out-- a proposal on June 6th by Senator James Inhofe to designate English as the official language of the United States. Just as he had one year prior, Barack Obama promptly voted against the amendment. [111] Now quite comfortable as a Senator with more than two years under his belt, Obama had no reason to conceal his intentions. Just like reputation in the Illinois legislature, Obama established a solid far left voting record within the chambers of the United States Senate. The only question that now remained was how far that record would influence his political ambition and how far that ambition would allow him to go.

***

"The absolute certain way of bringing this nation to ruin, or preventing all possibility of its continuing to be a nation at all, would be to permit it to become a tangle of squabbling nationalities. We have but one flag..."

- Theodore Roosevelt, American President

## BARACK OBAMA'S FAR LEFT AGENDA BEGINS TO SHOW

From his official announcement as a Presidential candidate in February of 2007 to his present day speeches, Barack Obama has not softened his hard left stance concerning the defense of American security and the preservation of American culture. On the contrary, he has reinforced his far left agenda with further steps to sell out American citizens. During a Democratic Presidential debate in November of 2007, Barack Obama was pressed about statements he made concerning his support for drivers licenses to illegal immigrants. He stated, "When I was a state senator in Illinois I voted to require that illegal aliens get trained, get a license, get insurance, to protect public safety..." [112]

Asked again by CNN's Wolf Blitzer if as President he would support licenses for illegal immigrants, Obama replied, "I am not proposing that that's what we do... I support the notion that we have to deal with public safety and that drivers licenses at the state level could make that happen..." [113] With bursts of amusement beginning to emit from the crowd, Blitzer pressed the issue again, asking Obama the same question for a third time. Perhaps sensing the crowd growing weary of his antics, Obama finally answered, "Yes... But I am going to be fighting for comprehensive immigration reform..." [114]

With the gap between himself and hard working Americans continuing to widen, Barack Obama established himself as the candidate of disorder; committed to putting illegal immigrants ahead of American citizens.

# THE ROOTS OF THE ILLEGAL IMMIGRATION MOVEMENT

Obama drew strong criticism from political pundits of both parties when he addressed the National Council of La Raza in July of 2007 at its annual conference. Discussing his connection with the crowd regarding immigration and culture, Obama stated, "You know where I'm coming from because you know where I've been… I will not walk away from the 12 million undocumented immigrants who live and work and contribute to our country every day…" [115]

The "La Raza" movement represents the definitive battle for American security, American law, and American culture. La Raza is translated as, "The Race," and the La Raza movement is possibly the most dangerous collaboration of radical groups facing the preservation of American society today. Where the problem exists is mainly with American citizens not knowing what La Raza really is and what it stands for.

In his speech to the Senate floor on April 3rd, 2006, Barack Obama made mention of the hundreds of thousands of protestors marching through the streets of Chicago and Los Angeles. It was these very rallies that caught the attention of the late Georgia Congressman Charlie Norwood. Compelled to inform the American people of the true nature of the La Raza movement, Norwood took it upon himself to pen a letter to the conservative magazine, *Human Events*. [116] The letter set off a back and forth between Norwood and the National Council of La Raza concerning the organization's agenda and what the La Raza movement truly stood for.

La Raza itself is not an official organization, and should not be confused with the National Council of La Raza. The National Council of La Raza proclaims itself as the most mainstream of the groups comprising the La Raza movement and even receives millions of dollars in federal funding each year. This is despite the fact it continues to lobby US lawmakers for open borders and amnesty for illegal aliens.

The La Raza movement is a collection of groups formed to promote one radical agenda, engrained in racist motivation and anti-American sentiment. Perhaps the most well known group is the Movimiento Esutdiantil Chicano de Aztlan, better known as MEChA. If groups such as the National Council of La Raza are deemed moderate, then groups like MEChA more than make up for it.

MEChA has an unknown number of chapters at colleges and universities nationwide, with some estimates ranging as high as 1,000. The group continues to promote the principles of the La Raza movement today, with one such principle being "El Plan Espiritual de Aztlan," or Spiritual Plan for Aztlan.

The plan teaches that Arizona, California, Colorado, New Mexico, Oregon, Texas, Utah, and parts of Washington State comprise an area known as "Aztlan" -- a fictional homeland of the Aztec Indians before Europeans arrived in North America. This ideology is still taught today, and features prominently on a number of MEChA chapter websites at universities across the country. A statement from a past MEChA chapter at the University of Texas reads, "...We, the Chicano inhabitants and civilizers of the northern land of Aztlan... declare that the call of our blood is our power, our responsibility, and our inevitable destiny. ... Aztlan belongs to those who plant the seeds, water the fields, and gather the crops and not to the foreign Europeans. ... We are a bronze people with a bronze culture. Before the world, before all of North America, before all our brothers in the bronze continent, we are a nation, we are a union of free pueblos, we are Aztlan. For La Raza todo. Fuera de La Raza nada." [117]

The closing two-sentence motto is chilling to those who value American law and the defense of American culture against illegal immigration. Translated, the slogan means, "For The Race everything. Outside The Race, nothing." Despite the overwhelming evidence outlining the racist and anti-American elements involved in the La Raza movement, Barack Obama has refused to distance himself from their vitriolic hate speech. In July of 2008, Obama spoke at the NCLR's National Conference in San Diego, California, making it clear he has no intentions of ending his support for those willing to undermine the American rule of law and disregard those citizens whom have helped establish it.

## Neither Truth, Nor Justice, Nor the American Way

Speaking at a fundraiser in Fort Lauderdale, Florida in May of 2008, Barack Obama lashed out at critics of illegal immigration, accusing them of creating an environment hostile to immigration reform. He took specific aim at two of the better-known media personalities. Obama exclaimed, "A certain segment has basically been feeding a kind of xenophobia. There's a reason why hate crimes against Hispanic people doubled last year. If you have people like Lou Dobbs and Rush Limbaugh ginning things up, it's not surprising that would happen." [118]

Though one cannot be certain why Obama chose to focus on those two individuals, the problem comes not with his lecture topic, but rather his arithmetic. According to the Federal Bureau of Investigation, Obama's statistics are completely false. Incidents against Hispanics designated as "hate crimes," did not increase. With 2007 statistics still being compiled, the most recent full year of data is 2006.

By examining the FBI's Uniform Crime Report, we see a very different picture than what Barack Obama tried to paint. While it is true that from 2005 to 2006, hate crimes labeled by the FBI as "against Hispanics" did rise, it rose by less than 100 victims. This represents an increase of approximately 13%, substantially lower than the increase Obama claimed. By comparison three other demographics actually experienced a greater rise in the number of victims than did Hispanics.

According to the FBI, victims of incidents labeled as hate crimes increased 17% against Jews, 22% against homosexuals, and 38% against Muslims. 2006 statistics show that more whites were the victims of hate crimes than were Hispanics.

| Victims | 2004 | 2005 | 2006 | # | % |
|---------|------|------|------|---|---|
| Whites | 1,027 | 975 | 1,054 | 79 | 8% |
| Homosexuals | 1,428 | 1,162 | 1412 | 250 | 22% |
| Blacks | 3,475 | 3,322 | 3,332 | 10 | less 1% |
| Jews | 1,076 | 977 | 1,144 | 167 | 17% |
| Muslims | 201 | 151 | 208 | 57 | 38% |
| Hispanics | 646 | 722 | 819 | 97 | 13% [119] |

So did Barack Obama gain anything in fabricating numbers for an audience eager to hear a specific agenda? Though his intentions that night may never be known, according to press reports, the Obama campaign collected more than $500,000 at the event from approximately 800 donors. His casualty with the truth did not appear to hinder his fundraising efforts.

***

"Guard against the impostures of pretended patriotism."

- General George Washington, American President

## DEFENDING THE REPUBLIC

As the nation stands poised to elect new leadership, it is apparent that leader cannot be Barack Obama. Willing to counter the system of law and justice upon which our nation was founded, Obama will lead America down a dangerous path. He will further deteriorate American culture and identity. Make no mistake; Barack Obama is no American patriot. As we continue to debate the role of the United States within our world, we must remember the philosophies and actions that have taken us to the heights we remain at today.

We must recall the decisions and actions which allowed us to serve as the beacon of light in an otherwise darkened world. Let us never forget it was America, a nation conceived in liberty, founded in civilized thought, and unified in language; that served as the last best hope for mankind.

87   Mike Volpe, "Senator Obama Responds Vis a Vis the Dream Act," *The Provocateur*, http://theeprovocateur.blogspot.com/2007/12/few-days-ago-i-received-email-from.html (23 December 2007).

88   "Full Text of HB0060," *Illinois General Assembly*, http://www.ilga.gov/legislation/fulltext.asp?DocName=&SessionId=3&GA=93&DocTypeId=HB&DocNum=60&GAID=3&LegID=195&SpecSess=&Session=.

89   "Immigration Impact: Illinois," *Federation for American Immigration Reform*, http://www.fairus.org/site/PageServer?pagename=research_researche21f.

90   Jack Martin, "Breaking the Piggy Bank: How Illegal Immigration is Sending Schools into the Red," *The Federation for American Immigration Reform*, http://www.fairus.org/site/PageServer?pagename=research_researchf6ad.

91   "Full Text of SB0030," *Illinois General Assembly*, http://www.ilga.gov/legislation/fulltext.asp?DocName=&SessionId=3&GA=93&DocTypeId=HB&DocNum=60&GAID=3&LegID=195&SpecSess=&Session=.

92   "Uniform Crime Reports," *Illinois State Police*, http://www.isp.state.il.us/crime/ucrhome.cfm

93   "Full Text of SB0679," *Illinois General Assembly*, http://www.ilga.gov/legislation/fulltext.asp?DocName=&SessionId=3&GA=93&DocTypeId=SB&DocNum=679&GAID=3&LegID=3347&SpecSess=&Session.

94   "Full Text of SB0680," *Illinois General Assembly*, http://www.ilga.gov/legislation/fulltext.asp?DocName=&SessionId=3&GA=93&DocTypeId=SB&DocNum=680&GAID=3&LegID=3348&SpecSess=&Session.

95   "Full Text of SB0680," *Illinois General Assembly*, http://www.ilga.gov/legislation/fulltext.asp?DocName=&SessionId=3&GA=93&DocTypeId=SB&DocNum=680&GAID=3&LegID=3348&SpecSess=&Session.

96   "Full Text of SB0680," *Illinois General Assembly*, http://www.ilga.gov/legislation/fulltext.asp?DocName=&SessionId=3&GA=93&DocTypeId=SB&DocNum=680&GAID=3&LegID=3348&SpecSess=&Session.

97   Raymond Hernandez & Christopher Drew, "It's Not Just 'Ayes' and

'Nays': Obama's Votes in Illinois Echo" *New York Times,* http://www. nytimes.com/2007/12/20/us/politics/20obama.html (20 December 2007).

[98] *Newsweek Magazine,* 3 January 2007.

[99] "S.1033 Secure America and Orderly Immigration Act (Introduced in Senate)," *The Library of Congress,* http://thomas.loc.gov/home/ c109query.html.

[100] "S.1033 Secure America and Orderly Immigration Act (Introduced in Senate), "*The Library of Congress,* http://thomas.loc.gov/home/ c109query.html.

[101] "S.1033 Secure America and Orderly Immigration Act (Introduced in Senate)," *The Library of Congress,* http://thomas.loc.gov/home/ c109query.html.

[102] "S. 2611 Comprehensive Immigration Reform Act of 2006 Immigration Act (Engrossed or Agreed to or Passed by Senate)," *The Library of Congress,* http://thomas.loc.gov/home/c109query.html.

[103] "Floor Statement of Senator Barack Obama on Immigration Reform," *Barack Obama U.S. Senator for Illinois,* http://obama.senate.gov/ speech/060403-floor_statement_3/ (3 April 2006).

[104] "Floor Statement of Senator Barack Obama on Immigration Reform," *Barack Obama U.S. Senator for Illinois,* http://obama.senate.gov/ speech/060403-floor_statement_3/ (3 April 2006).

[105] Michelle Malkin, *The American Flag Comes Second,* http://michellemalkin.com/2006/03/29/the-american-flag-comes-second/ (29 May 2006).

[106] "On the Amendment (Inhofe Amdt. No. 4064)," *United States Senate,* http://www.senate.gov/legislative/LIS/roll_call_lists/roll_call_vote_cfm. cfm?congress=109&session=2&vote=00131.

[107] http://www.us-english.org/.

[108] "S.Amdt. 4072 to S. 2611 Comprehensive Immigration Reform Act of 2006 Immigration Act (Engrossed or Agreed to or Passed by Senate)," *The Library of Congress,* http://thomas.loc.gov/home/c109query.html.

[109]  "S. 2611 Comprehensive Immigration Reform Act of 2006 Immigration Act (Engrossed or Agreed to or Passed by Senate)," *The Library of Congress,* http://thomas.loc.gov/home/c109query.html.

[110]  "On Passage of the Bill (S. 2611 As Amended)," *United States Senate,* http://www.senate.gov/legislative/LIS/roll_call_lists/roll_call_vote_cfm.cfm?congress=109&session=2&vote=00157.

[111]  "Declaring English the National Language," *Project Vote Smart,* http://votesmart.org/issue_keyvote_member.php?cs_id=13429.

[112]  "Barack Obama: Driver's licenses for illegal immigrants," *YouTube,* http://www.youtube.com/watch?v=CNvdOYl63q0 (16 November 2007).

[113]  Ibid.

[114]  Ibid.

[115]  "Barack Obama at La Raza Conference," *YouTube,* http://www.youtube.com/watch?v=aEITOQfKVmo (7 August 2007).

[116]  Rep. Charlie Norwood, "Exclusive: The Truth About 'La Raza'." *Human Events,* http://www.humanevents.com/article.php?id=13863 (7 April 2006).

[117]  "El Plan De Aztlan," *Mecha de Tejaztlan* http://studentorgs.utexas.edu/mecha/archive/index_old.html (30 April 1998).

[118]  Newsmax Staff, "Obama: Limbaugh, Lou Dobbs Spur Latino Hate," *Newsmax* http://www.newsmax.com/insidecover/Obama_Limbaugh_Dobbs/2008/05/23/98418.html (23 May 2008).

[119]  "2006 Hate Crime Statistics" *Federal Bureau of Investigation,* http://www.fbi.gov/ucr/hc2006/index.html.

# CHAPTER 5

## BARACK OBAMA VERSUS THE AMERICAN FAMILY

Despite Obama's efforts to publicly portray himself as a post-partisan, moderate bridge-builder, especially on social issues, his voting record illuminates the nature of his radical liberal beliefs. For example, as an Illinois state Senator, Obama voted against filtering pornography on elementary school library computers. In 2000, Obama voted "present" on a bill which would notify parents when their minor children seek an abortion. In addition, he twice voted against bills prohibiting the tax funding of abortions. He not only wants to keep abortion legal, but wants taxpayers to fund this controversial procedure that more than half of Americans equate to murder. In 2001, Barack Obama voted "present" on a bill to keep pornographic book stores, video stores, and strip clubs from setting up within 1,000 feet of schools and churches. In 2007, he said he would support voting for "sex education" for kindergarten children. Barack Obama also voted against a cloning ban in 2000 and touts the fact that he is an advocate for so-called "same-sex marriages."[120]

Most shockingly, not only does Obama support partial birth abortion, he voted against protecting babies who survive these late-term abortions. While Obama was still a state senator in Illinois, the United States Senate considered legislation to require that babies who survive abortion are cared for. In 2002, the Born-Alive Infants Protection Act passed the U.S. Senate without opposition. Not even Barbara Boxer, the U.S.

Senate's chief abortion advocate, opposed this bill. Around the same time, similar legislation was introduced in the Illinois State Senate. Did State Senator Barack Obama vote to protect these abortion-surviving children? Absolutely not. Apparently Barack Obama found nothing disturbing about an abortion procedure in which labor is induced to birth a child prematurely and then the baby is left to suffer and die without any care or attention. Furthermore, Obama refused to allow the Health and Human Services Committee that he chaired to even consider a later version of the bill.[121]

Obama's abortion position is so extreme that he is actually more pro-abortion than NARAL Pro-Choice America (formerly the National Abortion Rights Action League). Even NARAL did not oppose the Born-Alive Infants Protection Act. When the federal bill was being debated, NARAL released the following statement that said, "Consistent with our position last year, NARAL does not oppose the passage of the Born Alive Infants Protection Act ... floor debate served to clarify the bill's intent and assure us that it is not targeted at *Roe v. Wade* or a woman's right to choose."[122] When Obama tries to take a centrist view of abortion in public, or seems to oppose some abortions, as he has already tried to do in his Presidential campaign, we must remember the facts of his radically pro-abortion voting record.

Obama has even promised Planned Parenthood that he "will not yield" on his pro-abortion position.[123] "With one more vacancy on the [Supreme] Court, we could be looking at a majority hostile to a woman's fundamental right to choose for the first time since Roe versus Wade and that is what is at stake in this election," Obama told an audience at a Planned Parenthood conference on July 17, 2007. "I have worked on these issues for decades now," he said. "I put Roe at the center of my lesson plan on reproductive freedom when I taught Constitutional Law. Not simply as a case about privacy but as part of the broader struggle for women's equality."[124] Obama is clear: he has no intention to compromise his pro-abortion position.

At that same Planned Parenthood conference, Obama said that sex education for kindergarteners is "the right thing to do."[125] Obama believes that the state should be in the business of providing "age-appropriate sex education, science-based sex education in schools." He would rather not leave this responsibility to a child's family, even at that tender age when children are barely learning how to read and write.

In March of 2008, while on the campaign trail, Obama went on further about what we should teach our children as they progress through the government school system:

> When it comes specifically to HIV/AIDS, the most important prevention is education, which should include -- which should include abstinence education and teaching the children -- teaching children, you know, that sex is not something casual. But it should also include -- it should also include other, you know, information about contraception because, look, I've got two daughters. 9 years old and 6 years old. I am going to teach them first of all about values and morals. But if they make a mistake, I don't want them punished with a baby. I don't want them punished with an STD at the age of 16. You know, so it doesn't make sense to not give them information.[126]

While we can disagree about how our children should learn about sexual reproduction and the role of the state in passing on that education to children, this statement by Obama, combined with his other views on abortion, partial-birth abortion, and the protections granted to infants who survive abortion, provide a glimpse inside the mind of Senator Obama and his views about the dignity of life at its very infancy. Most Americans and people around the world joyfully welcome babies into their lives and I imagine Obama welcomed his two daughters with joy as well. But in this statement, Obama revealed his progressive views as he described these most innocent human beings as a "punishment," and equated an unexpected child to an unexpected disease such as an STD.

By now, it ought to be easy to see where the nation's most liberal senator stands on issues related to the family. To be precise, Barack Obama received a score of "absolutely zero" by the Family Research Council's

*Family Action Voter's Guide*, which rates all congressional members' voting records on family-related legislation. Upon the release of the *Family Action Voter's Guide*, Family Research Council president Tony Perkins, cognizant of Barack Obama's silver tongue, advised supporters of the family to look at the candidate's records and past performances rather than to allow 30-second commercials to, "Tug at your heart strings."[127]

Obama's high voltage voting record is obviously shocking and raises weighty questions like, "why would kindergarteners need 'sex education'?" "Why would someone allow newborns to be left to die?" and "Why would a politician who identifies as a Christian advocate for so-called "same-sex marriage"? Does his far left voting record represent the type of "change" that most Americans are looking for, or, are most Americans looking for a candidate who will support more traditional family values?

To answer, we may look to the book, *The American Way*, where author Allan Carlson begins by noting that in the fall of 1999, "the Wirthlin Worldwide polling organization conducted an international survey regarding social values. Nearly 2,900 randomly selected persons in five global regions responded to the following question: 'If you could create a society the way you think it should be, what would that society be centered around?' The choices offered were family, government, business, church, and individual."[128]

"The results of the survey were surprising. In the United States, fully 67 percent of persons chose 'family' and another 20 percent chose 'church.' If we add these numbers together to form a kind of 'communitarian index,' the figure of 87 percent is as close to unanimous as polling usually gets. The U.S. participants, moreover, chose "family" and "church" more than did those in any other region of the world. In Europe for example, 58 percent chose 'family' and only 4 percent chose 'church.' Only 8 percent of Americans would build their society around the 'individual.' 'Business' was the choice of a mere 3 percent and 'government' was the choice of 2 percent. In sum, nearly 9 out of 10 Americans in 1999 claimed to believe that social order should be centered around families and religious communities."[129]

It appears then, that when it comes to traditional family values, Barack Obama is not offering the type of "change" that nearly all Americans are looking for. The consensus among citizens of this Republic is solidly in favor of the traditional family and for good reason. The family is where most Americans believe we ought to start because the family is where we all, in fact, do start. As noted in the recently republished book *Family and Civilization*, human experience points us in the direction of the family. Harvard sociologist Carle Zimmerman notes that:

No problem is more interesting and vital to us than that of the family. The child is born into a family and sees the world through its eyes. His introduction to civilization is through the family. At first he is only a child in a system of social relations consisting of a unity of husband and wife, parent and child. Later he learns that there are relatives (grandmothers, aunts, uncles, cousins, etc.) who are closer to him than other people. In time he acquires the idea of friends, and then of strangers. Then he learns that he secures his status through his family. He is an American, an Englishman, a Chinese because he is born into a parental unit that belongs to those nationalities. His parents belong to a certain community and so does he, and they are subject to its rules and privileges. He can and must go to the schools of his community. As the child grows up, he founds a family of his own where the roles are reversed; instead of remaining a child, he becomes a husband (wife), parent, leader, breadwinner, responsible person, disciplinarian, and status conferrer. In the course of a lifetime, most people play changing roles within the organization known as the family.[130]

It seems self-evident that the center and progenitor of our lives and civilization is the family, and marriage is the cement of every healthy and well-ordered family. Marriage, in the words of pro-family advocate Jennifer Roback Morse, "is society's normative institution for both sexual activity and child rearing."[131] Marriage is an organic pre-political institution that emerges spontaneously from society, says Morse. "Government does not create families any more than the government creates jobs. Just as people have a natural propensity to 'truck, barter, and exchange one thing for another,' in Adam Smith's famous words from the second chapter of *The Wealth of Nations*, we likewise have a natural tendency to couple, procreate, and rear children. People instinctively create families, both as couples and as a culture, without any support from the government whatsoever."[132]

The alternative to the view of marriage asserted here, as a naturally occurring, pre-political institution is the progressive view, like Barack Obama's, which defines marriage as a strict creation of the state, as if marriage could be created out of whole cloth and reinvented at will. So-called "no-fault divorce," "same-sex marriage," "polygamous marriage," "polyandrous marriage," are necessarily not only ad hoc and whimsical institutions, they are in actual fact, meaningless combinations of words; unintelligible statements. Such phrases do not even rise to the dignity of error and if accepted, by definition, mean the abolition of marriage. Marriage as a formal institution will have been defined out of existence.

Obama argues that civil unions for same-sex couples shouldn't be a "lesser thing" than marriage.[133] If this view is true, however, then as has been noted, the principle upon which it stands also says that the state can recreate marriage in any form it chooses. Implicit in this view is not only the abolition of marriage but the illusion that the state is the ultimate source of social order.

To provide some background on why it is that those on the far left hold such views about marriage, listen to a self-described "progressive" bring the implicit connection between the expansive state and the deconstruction of marriage out of the shadows. New York University Queer Studies Professor Lisa Duggan critiques the marriage promotion portion of welfare reform:

> Women and children... [according to the welfare reform model] should depend on men for basic economic support, while women care for dependents—children, elderly parents, disabled family members, etc. Under such a model-couple households might "relieve" the state of the expense of helping to support single-parent households, and for the cost of a wide range of social services, from childcare and disability services to home nursing. Marriage thus becomes a

privatization scheme: Individual married-couple households give women and children access to higher men's wages, and also, "privately" provide many services once offered through social welfare agencies. More specifically, the unpaid labor of married women fills the gap created by government service cuts.[134]

This statement brings the statist world view of liberals like Obama out of the closet. The modern progressive view believes that the most basic relationships are not those between husband and wife, parent and child, but between individuals and the state. They believe that the family is not the natural unit of society. For them, the most basic unit of society is not even the libertarian individual, embedded within a complex web of family, business, and social relationships. Rather, the natural unit of society is the naked individual, the isolated individual, standing alone before the state, dependent upon the state.[135]

Describing marriage as a "privatization scheme" implies that the most desirable way to care for a dependent is for the state to provide care. This view seems to be implicit in recent liberal attempts to offer state-sponsored pre-schools and state-sponsored universal health care. An appreciation of voluntary cooperation between men and women, young and old, weak and strong, so natural to the American way, is completely absent from the progressive world view.

This is why it is no accident that the advocates of laissez-faire sexuality, like Barack Obama, are among the most vociferous opponents of laissez-faire economics. Advocates of so-called "same-sex marriage" are quick to point out that civil marriage confers more than 1,049 automatic federal and additional state protections, benefits and responsibilities, according to the federal government's General Accounting Office.[136]   If these governmentally bestowed benefits and responsibilities are indeed the core of marriage, then this package should be equally available to all citizens. It follows that these benefits of marriage should be available to any grouping of individuals, and any size or combination of genders, of any degree of permanence.

The American political tradition does not start with the belief that what the government chooses to bestow or withhold is the essence of any social institution. When we hear students from other countries naively ask, "If the government doesn't create jobs, how will we ever have any jobs?" most Americans know how to respond. Just because the government employs people and gives away tax money does not mean it "created" jobs. Likewise, the fact that the government gives away bundles of goodies to married couples does not prove that the government created marriage.[137]

Granted, the state may still need to protect, encourage, or support permanence in married couples, just as the state may need to support the sanctity of contracts. The presumption of laissez-faire economics means that the government cannot ignore violations of property rights, contracts, or fair exchange. Enforcing laws and contracts is one of the basic functions of government. With these standards for economic behavior in place, Americans can create wealth and pursue their own interests with little or no additional assistance from the state. Likewise, formal and informal standards and sanctions create the context in which couples can create marriage, with minimal assistance from the state.[138]

\*\*\*

Obama's church, Trinity United Church of Christ in Chicago, has supported "same-sex marriage" since 2005. Obama is on board. In a 2004 letter to a gay Chicago newspaper, the *Windy City Times*, Obama voiced his support for so-called "same-sex marriage," when he stated, "I opposed the Defense of Marriage Act in 1996. It should be repealed and I will vote for its repeal on the Senate floor. I will also oppose any proposal to amend the U.S. Constitution to ban gays and lesbians from marrying."[139] Obama once referred to a televised forum focusing on same-sex attraction as "a historic moment ... for America."[140] Obama has stated that he wants to tap into the "core decency" of Americans to fight discrimination against gays and lesbians, and he has argued that civil unions for same-sex couples shouldn't be a "lesser thing" than marriage. While no American should be discriminated against, neither should the state "redefine" marriage by "giving" special rights.

Throughout his book, *The Audacity of Hope*, and in many of his speeches, Obama attempts to portray the "Religious Right" as an entity which simply tries to make the important social issues of family, human life, abortion, sex education, and marriage "wedge" issues between Republicans and Democrats. He claims that the "Religious Right" simply uses these issues to win votes and distract Americans from other issues. Perhaps Obama does not understand the history of the "pro-family" movement in this country, which began in reaction to the imposition of progressive values on the traditional beliefs shared by almost all Americans. Beginning in the 1960s and 1970s, progressives began to use the state, mostly through the courts, to overturn historic social institutions that have upheld the moral fabric of our nation for more than two centuries.

"Social conservatives," writes Obama in *The Audacity of Hope*, "want a return to a bygone era, in which sexuality outside marriage was subject to both punishment and shame, obtaining a divorce was far more difficult, and marriage offered not merely personal fulfillment but also well-defined social roles for men and women. In their view," he writes, "any government policy that appears to reward or even express neutrality toward what they consider to be immoral behavior—whether providing birth control to young people, abortion services to women, welfare support to unwed mothers, or legal recognition of same-sex unions—inherently devalues the marital bond."[141]

Here, Barack Obama divulges his position on social issues with spectacular brevity. What I would like to highlight, however, is his belief that it is the proper role of the state to reward or at least express neutrality toward certain behaviors. Today, however, it seems that a motivated but radical fringe group of Americans on the far left have forgotten or rejected the definition of the word "marriage." They argue that any type of relationship, so long as it is "adult and consensual," ought to be considered a "marriage" by society. The ideology of relativism leads progressives to believe that they can just change the definition of words and institutions such as marriage. 2007's "most liberal" U.S. Senator, Barack Obama, can be considered among such persons, and some of Obama's votes and statements already outlined in this chapter provide a psychological keyhole, through which we might have a peek at the views that lie behind the candidate's voting record.

Obama's views on these important social issues are often not in line with Christian teachings, but that has not stopped him from staking his own claim on such issues. In a supposed dispute with Christian leaders, Obama defends his anti-Christian views on abortion, same-sex unions, and other family-related issues. "Democracy," he writes,

> ...demands that the religiously motivated translate their concerns into universal, rather than religion-specific, values. It requires that their proposals be subject to argument, and amenable to reason. I may be opposed to abortion for religious reasons, but if I seek to pass a law banning the practice, I cannot simply point to the teachings of my church or evoke God's will. Now this is going to be difficult for some who believe in the inerrancy of the Bible, as many evangelicals do. But in a pluralistic democracy, we have no choice. Politics depends on our ability to persuade each other of common aims based on a common reality. It involves the compromise, the art of what's possible. At some fundamental level, religion does not allow for compromise. It's the art of the impossible."[142]

Obama even goes so far as to label those with traditional Christian views as intolerant. In 1995, he wrote that, "The right wing, the Christian right, has done a good job of building these organizations of accountability, much better than the left or progressive forces have. But it's always easier to organize around intolerance, narrow mindedness, and false nostalgia. And they also have high jacked higher moral ground with this language of family values and moral responsibility."[143]
"I don't think it [a same-sex union] should be called marriage, but I think that it is a legal right that they should have that is recognized by the state," said Obama in 2008. "If people find that controversial then I would just refer them to the Sermon on the Mount, which I think is, in my mind, for my faith, more central than an obscure passage in Romans," in which

Paul's Epistle to the Romans condemns homosexual acts as unnatural and sinful.[144]

Obama's mention of the Sermon on the Mount in justifying legal recognition of same-sex unions may have been a reference to the Golden Rule: "Do unto others what you would have them do to you." Or, it may have been a reference to another famous line in Jesus' sermon: "Do not judge, or you too will be judged." This is certainly a good point by the junior Senator, reminding us that we are all sinners in a fallen world. But, it is theologically incorrect and intellectually dishonest for anyone to pick and choose which part of the New Testament that a Christian should or should not follow. Christians are bound to follow it all. The Apostle Paul might be offended that a Christian such as Obama would call any part of his Letter to the Romans "an obscure passage." (We will jump into the Senator's religious faith in the next chapter).

***

Is Barack Obama's description of the traditional family, as belonging to a "bygone era," accurate? If it were, we would have to maintain that we would then be living in a "bygone civilization." It seems self-evident that as marriage goes, so goes the family, and as the family goes, so goes civilization.[145]

G.K. Chesterton once wrote that, "this triangle of truisms, of father, mother and child, cannot be destroyed; it can only destroy those civilizations which disregard it." In another place he wrote that, "The business done in the home is nothing less than the shaping of the bodies and souls of humanity. The family is the factory that manufactures mankind." The American family very well may be ailing, but it does not belong to a bygone civilization. It does, however, need leaders that respect the centrality of the family and the dignity of human life to strengthen the moral underpinnings of the nation. It does not need a President who will put activist judges on the highest courts in the land to reorder the traditional social institutions of America.

[120] Amanda Carpenter, "Obama's Voting Record Belies Moderate Image," *Human Events*, http://www.humanevents.com/article.php?id=18967, (16 January 2007).

[121] Amanda Carpenter, "Obama More Pro-Choice Than NARAL," *Human Events*, http://www.humanevents.com/article.php?id=18647, (12 December 2006).

[122] Ibid.

[123] Planned Parenthood is the nation's largest single abortion provider.

[124] "Obama pledged to Planned Parenthood: 'I will not yield' to pro-life concerns," *Catholic News Agency*, http://www.catholicnewsagency.com/new.php?n=11918, (28 February 2008).

[125] "Sex Ed for Kindergarteners 'Right Thing to Do,' Says Obama," *ABC News*, Political Radar, http://blogs.abcnews.com/politicalradar/2007/07/sex-ed-for-kind.html, (18 July 2007).

[126] David Brody, "Obama Says He Doesn't Want His Daughters 'Punished with a Baby'," *CBNNews.com*, http://www.cbn.com/CBNnews/348569.aspx, (31 March 2008).

[127] "Family Action Voter Guide," Family Research Council, http://www.frcaction.org.

[128] Allan Carlson, *The American Way* (Wilmington, DE: ISI Books, 2003), ix.

[129] Ibid

[130] Carle C. Zimmerman, *Family and Civilization* (Wilmington, DE: ISI Books, 2008), 1.

[131] Jennifer Roback Morse, "Marriage and the Limits of Contract," *Policy Review*, Hoover Institution, http://www.hoover.org/publications/policyreview/2939396.html, (April/May 2005).

[132] Ibid.

[133] Jill Lawrence, "Forum puts Democrats in hot seat over gay issues," *USA*

*Today*, http://www.usatoday.com/news/politics/election2008/2007-08-09-democrats-gay-forum_N.htm, (10 August 2007).

134 Lisa Duggan, "Holy Matrimony!" *The Nation*, http://www.thenation.com/doc/20040315/duggan/single, (26 February 2004).

135 Jennifer Roback Morse, *The Meaning of Marriage* (Dallas, TX: Spence Publishing, 2006), 86-88.

136 Jennifer Roback Morse, "Marriage and the Limits of Contract," *Policy Review*, Hoover Institution, http://www.hoover.org/publications/policyreview/2939396.html, (April/May 2005).

137 Jennifer Roback Morse, *The Meaning of Marriage*, 88.

138 Ibid.

139 "Obama on Marriage," *Windy City Times*, Letter from Barack Obama, http://www.windycitymediagroup.com/gay/lesbian/news/ARTICLE.php?AID=4018, (11 February 2004).

140 "Democratic contenders address gay rights in TV forum," *FOXNews.com*, http://www.foxnews.com/story/0,2933,292817,00.html?sPage=fnc/specialsections/issues, (10 August 2007).

141 Barack Obama, *The Audacity of Hope* (New York: Crown Publishers, 2006).

142 Barack Obama, "Politicians need not abandon religion," *USA Today*, http://www.usatoday.com/news/opinion/editorials/2006-07-09-forum-religion-obama_x.htm, (10 July 2006).

143 Hank De Zutter, "What Makes Obama Run?" *Chicago Reader*, http://www.chicagoreader.com/obama/951208, (8 December 1995).

144 Terence P. Jeffrey, "Obama: Sermon on Mount OKs Same-Sex Unions," *Newsmax*, http://www.newsmax.com/insidecover/Obama_same_sex/2008/03/03/77289.html, (3 March 2008).

145 Pope John Paul II once said, "As the family goes, so goes the nation and so goes the whole world in which we live."

# PART TWO: CHARACTER AND IDEOLOGY

# CHAPTER 6

## QUESTIONS OF FAITH:
## BARACK OBAMA'S RELIGIOUS EXPERIENCE

Barack Obama began his Presidential campaign on a religious footing. He has stressed how he wants to be a different candidate, the candidate of "change" that we have become so accustomed to hearing about. With this idea of "change," Obama also wanted to distinguish himself from his fellow Democrats and realign the political map. Part of this strategy is to win people of religious faith over to his side.

In more recent years, religion has been a deep divide in American politics. Polls show that voters who attend a religious service at least once a week are far more likely to vote for a Republican.[146] In 2004, the media demonstrated this over and over again with the way that President George W. Bush and his political advisor, Karl Rove, focused on turning out the religious vote for the President, a self-described evangelical Christian.

On October 7, 2007, Obama told an audience of Sunday worshippers at the Redemption World Outreach Center, "I think it's important, particularly for those of us in the Democratic Party, to not cede values and faith to any one party."[147] For a Christian of any political persuasion, this is certainly a welcome statement. But is it sincere? Is Barack Obama, like many politicians before him, simply trying to win over a constituency he so desperately needs to win not only his party's nomination, but ultimately the White House?

Before we proceed any further, let's dip back into Obama's history as it relates to his faith in order to bring us up to speed on how he got to this point in 2007.

## WAS OBAMA EVER A MUSLIM?

In the heat of the campaign for the Democrat nomination, reports began surfacing that Obama had attended a radical Islamic "madrassa" school, as a child in Indonesia. In January 2007, Obama's chief spokesperson, Robert Gibbs, denied this charge. He said that Obama was raised "in a secular household in Indonesia by his stepfather and mother."[148] He clarified further, "To be clear, Senator Obama has never been a Muslim, was not raised a Muslim, and is a committed Christian who attends the United Church of Christ in Chicago."

Yet, in a statement to the *Los Angeles Times*, just a few days before a March 16, 2007 story about the possibility of Obama's "Muslim past," the Obama campaign worded things slightly differently, saying: "Obama has never been a practicing Muslim." According to Paul Watson of the *Los Angeles Times*, "The statement added that as a child, Obama had spent time in the neighborhood's Islamic center" during his childhood in Indonesia.

> The *L.A. Times* story continues:
>
> His former Roman Catholic and Muslim teachers [in Indonesia], along with two people who were identified by Obama's grade school teacher as childhood friends, say Obama was registered by his family as a Muslim at both of the schools he attended.
>
> That registration meant that during the third and fourth grades, Obama learned about Islam for two hours each week in religion class.
>
> The childhood friends say Obama sometimes went to Friday prayers at the local mosque. "We prayed but not really seriously, just following actions done by older people in the mosque. But as kids, we loved to meet our

friends and went to the mosque together and prayed,"
said Zulfin Adi, who describes himself as among Obama's
closest childhood friends.

The clarification of Obama's campaign that he has never been a *practicing* Muslim was indeed a careful clarification. Judging from all accrued evidence – from Barack Obama's two books, his own statements (both personal and political), and from the records uncovered by credible journalists – the fact remains that Obama was born a Muslim and given a Muslim name: Barack Hussein Obama. The facts also seem to verify that he has never been a *practicing* Muslim.

\*\*\*

On December 22, 2007, Obama was on the Iowa campaign trail, having a quiet chat with four local ladies at the Smoky Row Coffee Shop.[149] When one woman asked him about his Muslim heritage, Obama replied with the following:

> My father was from Kenya, and a lot of people in his
> village were Muslim. He didn't practice Islam. Truth is
> he wasn't very religious. He met my mother. My mother
> was a Christian from Kansas, and they married and then
> divorced. I was raised by my mother. So, I've always been
> a Christian. The only connection I've had to Islam is
> that my grandfather on my father's side came from that
> country. But I've never practiced Islam. … For a while, I
> lived in Indonesia because my mother was teaching there.
> And that's a Muslim country. And I went to school. But I
> didn't practice.

As we will see later in this chapter, these very words from Obama to the four women in Iowa are revealing about how Obama has explained his religion. I'm not sure if he actually wrote his book, *The Audacity of Hope* (or read it), but in that book, he constructs a slightly different story.

His father was indeed from Kenya, as he mentions in his two books. In fact, Obama still has family in Kenya. In *The Audacity of Hope*, Obama says that "although my father had been raised a Muslim, by the time he met my mother he was a confirmed atheist, thinking religion to be so much superstition..."[150]

So far, the story in his book matches up with the story he gave the four women in the Iowa coffee shop. In fact, it seems those four Iowa women got a much fuller explanation about this part of his religious past than Obama even gave his readers in *The Audacity of Hope*. However, he told the four Iowa women that his mother was "a Christian from Kansas" and that he, Barack Obama, had "always been a Christian." Really? That's not quite the same story he constructs in *The Audacity of Hope*. Let's get *that* story, in Obama's own words (we think):

> My mother viewed religion through the eyes of the anthropologist that she would become; it [religion] was a phenomenon to be treated with a suitable respect, but with a suitable detachment as well.[151]

In *The Audacity of Hope*, Obama talks about his own "faith" story, in a lengthy chapter about how he came to his Christian faith. In that chapter, he details how his mother, Ann Dunham, was *raised* Christian, but by the time she was in college in the 1960s, she began to view religion "through the eyes of the anthropologist that she would become." His mother married Barack Obama Sr. According to Obama, his biological father, Barack Obama Sr., a Kenyan, was a non-practicing Muslim. It may not be relevant whether Obama's father was a Muslim. Obama didn't get to know his biological father very well, as Obama Sr. abandoned the family when Obama Jr. was only two years old.[152]

Senator Obama was born in Honolulu in 1961, while his mother was studying at the University of Hawaii. He was born to a Muslim and given a Muslim name. When Obama's mother remarried, it was to another student who she met at the University of Hawaii, Lolo Soetoro.[153]

Soetoro's student visa was revoked while he was at Hawaii and he traveled back to Indonesia, where he was conscripted into the Indonesian army. A few months later, in 1967, Obama and his mother arrived in Indonesia. Obama characterizes his stepfather's religious beliefs as one of a "skeptic," though it can be assumed his stepfather (like his biological father) was also a born Muslim, but perhaps not a practicing Muslim. Indonesia was "a Muslim country," as Obama himself told the four Iowa women. Today, it is the most populous Muslim country in the world.

At the age of six, Obama and his mother (who was 24) moved to Indonesia during very turbulent times for that country. In *The Audacity of Hope*, Obama claims his mother, who was living as a college student in the Pacific islands of Hawaii, didn't know about the trouble in Indonesia until she got there – due to lack of attention that Indonesia had received in the American media. Just two years before Obama and his mother arrived in Indonesia, nearly one million people had been slaughtered in the Suharto coup against the communist dictator Sukarno.

During Obama's five years in Indonesia, he lived with his mother and stepfather. In his book, he says he was first sent to "a neighborhood Catholic school" and "then to a predominantly Muslim school."[154] The *Los Angeles Times* story noted that Obama did not attend a radical Islamic "madrassa" school. The radical Islamic extremists were not as strong in the 1960s, when Obama was there, as they are today. But the *Times* also noted that the people Obama grew up with in Indonesia knew him as Barry Soetoro – not as Barack Obama. Soetoro, remember, was his stepfather's last name.

The *Times* spoke to Zulfin Adi, who described himself as among Obama's closest childhood friends. Adi told the *Times* that "[Obama's] mother often went to the church, but Barry [Barack Obama] was a Muslim. He went to the mosque, I remember him wearing a sarong."[155]

Obama's sister, who was born after the family moved to Indonesia, gave the following statement to the *L.A. Times*: "My father saw Islam as a way to connect with the community. He never went to prayer services except for big communal events. I am absolutely certain that my father did not go to services every Friday. He was not religious."

Obama tells us in his book that he grew up with the good values his mother taught him. While she remained secular, Obama has always considered her "spiritually awakened." She was still able to teach him the same values that most Americans learn in Sunday school, he says. But, as Obama details in *The Audacity of Hope*, it wasn't until after college, when Obama came into contact with Trinity United Church of Christ in Chicago while he was a political organizer in the community, that he became a Christian.

It was there – at Trinity United Church of Christ – where he first saw how there might be something more to religion than viewing it as just a custom. He personally saw how Christianity was transforming people's lives. He later converted and it was at Trinity United Church of Christ where he was first baptized and became a practicing Christian.

Does the "faith story" Obama constructed in his book match the "faith story" he described to the four Iowa women? He told them he had "always been a Christian." Yet, in his book he seems to try to first identify with atheists and secularists and then finally with Christians. His book constructs a wonderful story that can help a Democrat, such as Obama, reach out to those religious voters who typically vote Republican, while still being able to identify with the more typical Democrat voter who does not attend church regularly or take faith seriously. Is this a sincere story or a well constructed triangulation to win over the plurality of voters that a politician like Obama might need to win?

If it is sincere faith story, one has to wonder why he contradicted himself in that coffee shop by saying he had "always been a Christian." Based on the evidence, one could actually say Obama had really always been a Muslim. Born a Muslim and with a Muslim name, it is unclear whether Obama actually *practiced* Islam. But, what is clear is that it was false of him to state to those four women in Iowa that he had "always been a Christian."

## OBAMA BECOMES A CHRISTIAN

In *The Audacity of Hope*, Obama says that "he accepted work after college as a community organizer for a group of churches in Chicago that were trying to cope with joblessness, drugs, and hopelessness in their midst."[156] Obama was a young idealist, equipped with a Harvard law degree and with a passion for political organizing. He was also "searching for a tradition to be a part of," he said.

Obama was brought up to believe religion was empty, and was nothing more than a way people organized themselves as a community. His respect for religion, stemming from his mother's beliefs, was limited to view religion as solely a social construction. Naturally, to politically organize blacks in Chicago, he knew to look to the historically black churches.

Obama said he was "drawn to the power of the African American religious tradition to spur social change."[157] In other words, his first approach to these historically black churches in Chicago was a *political* one. Obama even acknowledges in his book that the historically black church "had to serve as the center of the community's political, economic, and social as well as spiritual life; to feed the hungry and clothe the naked and challenge powers and principalities."

He began to have a higher respect for Christianity because, as he put it, he began to see faith "as an active, palpable agent in the world." While working with people in the black Chicago community, he began to attend services at Trinity United Church of Christ. It was there, as noted earlier, that Obama was baptized and began a close relationship with his pastor, Dr. Jeremiah Wright. Obama's entire institutional experience with Christianity has been guided by this church and by this pastor.

From the outset of his campaign, Obama's relationship to Dr. Wright has been examined. The church has been accused of being "racist" because of its emphasis on a "black power liberation theology." Part of this criticism stemmed from the church's own website and the statement that it has chosen to describe itself by:

> We are a congregation which is Unashamedly Black and
> Unapologetically Christian... Our roots in the Black
> religious experience and tradition are deep, lasting and
> permanent. We are an African people, and remain "true
> to our native land," the mother continent, the cradle
> of civilization. God has superintended our pilgrimage
> through the days of slavery, the days of segregation,
> and the long night of racism. It is God who gives us the
> strength and courage to continuously address injustice
> as a people, and as a congregation. We constantly affirm
> our trust in God through cultural expression of a Black
> worship service and ministries which address the Black
> Community.[158]

Some members of the media picked up on this statement that looks similar to a Black Nationalist or black separatist group. With the statements "Unashamedly Black", "we are an African people ..." and "we constantly affirm our trust in God through cultural expression of a Black worship service and ministries which address the Black community," some have called these statements racist or examples of "reverse racism."

They say: if we reversed these words and applied it to a white supremacist church that said they were "unashamedly white" or that they were a "Caucasian people" that "found our cultural expression in a White worship service which addressed the White community," there would be an outrage on the scale of Don Imus. There most certainly would. I can hear Al Sharpton and Jesse Jackson screaming now.

But, there are hundreds of such historically black churches around this country. It is ultimately up to each of those churches to define who they are and how they want to identify with the rest of the American community, based on their historical and religious experiences.

The point I want to raise here in this chapter is the other side of Trinity United Church of Christ. In fact, in response to their church becoming the target of so much scrutiny, the church put some YouTube style videos on their website to demonstrate how "inclusive" they actually are. Trinity has a white female minister, Jane Fisler Hoffman. In the video on their website, Hoffman says that Trinity is a "radically welcoming church." After a little review, we'll find her statement that this church is "radically welcoming" contains more truth than we originally thought.

***

On March 1, 2007, Dr. Jeremiah Wright appeared on Fox News' *Hannity & Colmes* television program to respond to critics of his church. To explain his church's beliefs, Dr. Wright said that Trinity United Church of Christ was founded on "the Black Value system which was developed by this congregation, by lay persons of this congregation 26 years ago, very similar to the gospel [INAUDIBLE] developed by lay persons in Nicaragua during the whole liberation theology movement 26, 28, 30 years ago."[159]

Now it's time to pay attention. This is where this church's beliefs *really* get interesting.

## THE LIBERATION THEOLOGY MOVEMENT

Before we proceed any further, we need a fuller explanation of liberation theology. Dr. Wright insisted to Sean Hannity that he needed to learn about this theology. For us to understand Trinity United Church of Christ, its politics, and perhaps the politics of the Presidential candidate that has attended this church for nearly 20 years, we should learn what the foundations of this church's views are.

Volumes have been written on the subject of liberation theology over the past few decades, but I will be as brief as I can here.

Liberation theology began as a school of theology within the Catholic Church in 1955 and really started taking off in the 1960s and 1970s, spreading within Catholicism but also permeating into many other Protestant denominations. Liberation theology focuses on Jesus Christ as not only the *redeemer* but also the *liberator* of the oppressed. It emphasizes the Christian mission to bring justice to the poor and the oppressed.

While liberation theology certainly shines a light on the Christian responsibility of helping the poor, it does not stop there. It merges this theology with political activism, particularly in the areas of social justice, poverty, and human rights. Liberation theology is still a force within the Roman Catholic Church even though it is only partially compatible with official statements of Catholic social teaching. Large portions of this theology have been rejected by the Vatican, including by Popes John Paul II and Benedict XVI.

Most of the objections to liberation theology by the Catholic Church and other Christian churches are of its uses of Marxism, specifically forms of dialectical materialism, and some tendencies to align with revolutionary movements. Dialectical materialism is the philosophical root of Marxism and is basically characterized by the notion that all of history is one of class struggle.

Before he was Pope Benedict XVI, Cardinal Joseph Ratzinger was head of the Congregation of the Doctrine of the Faith, which is the office within the Vatican that oversees Catholic doctrine. After much study and investigation, Cardinal Ratzinger came to view liberation theology as heretical and issued a statement on this subject in the "Preliminary notes" to his *Instruction* on the Catholic faith in 1984. In these notes, Ratzinger said, "An analysis of the phenomenon of liberation theology reveals that it constitutes a fundamental threat to the faith of the Church. At the same time it must be borne in mind that no error could persist unless it contained a grain of truth. Indeed, an error is all the more dangerous, the greater that grain of truth is, for then the temptation it exerts is all the greater."[160]

In other words, Ratzinger viewed liberation theology as a "great threat" precisely because it contained a "grain of truth" (notably, the Christian responsibility to serve the poor). The greatest heresies, after all, are the ones that contain the most truth. The "greater that grain of truth is," the more likely we are to believe it even if it is not compatible with the totality of church teaching. This ideology of liberation theology has swept up many converts over the past few decades because it has played into the Christian belief to serve the poor. But, it has taken this belief to new ends.

While liberation theology began within the Catholic Church, it has not been alien to Protestant churches. In fact, many liberal Protestant churches, including in the United States, have inherited this ideology as well. One of those churches is Trinity United Church of Christ in Chicago.

To be clear, the full mantra of liberation theology does not sit well with the Roman Catholic Church or any mainline Christian Church. Mostly because, as Cardinal Ratzinger has said, "liberation theology intends to supply a new total interpretation of the Christian reality." In addition, Ratzinger pointed out that from the view of liberation theologians, "all reality is political, liberation is also a political concept and the guide to liberation must be a guide to political action." Furthermore, Ratzinger added:

> A theologian who has learned his theology in the classical
> tradition and has accepted its spiritual challenge will
> find it hard to realize that an attempt is being made
> [by liberation theology], in all seriousness, to recast the
> whole Christian reality in the categories of politico-social
> liberation praxis. This is all the more difficult because
> many liberation theologians continue to use a great deal
> of the Church's classical ascetical and dogmatic language
> while changing its signification. As a result, the reader or
> listener who is operating from a different background can

gain the impression that everything is the same as before, apart from the addition of a few somewhat unpalatable statements, which, given so much spirituality, can scarcely be all that dangerous.

Liberation theology, in a nutshell, is so dangerous because it goes further than just the Christian call to serve the poor. It calls for political action and merges politics and theology. In some cases, it goes further and calls for revolutionary action, even if that action must be violent.

Marxism, as an ideology, was originally built on a foundation of atheism. Marxists typically are anti-religion because they see religion as the instrument by which the powerful elite have "moved the masses" for their own interests. Marxists do not believe in God or an afterlife, and thus they see a clear injustice when they view the poor, the working class, and a capitalist system that does not produce equality in the here and now.

What is different about liberation theology is that it merges the materialism of Marxism into Christianity. Rather than rejecting the materialism of both capitalism and Marxism, which is more in line with Christian social teaching, liberation theology accepts the materialist arguments of Marxism. Thus, this "theology" has fed many violent revolutions in Latin America and Asia, as liberation theologians and their followers merged with communist revolutionaries.

Today, the threat of communism has quieted, but liberation theology still persists in other forms. One such thread of liberation theology was developed by James Cone, the very author who Jeremiah Wright cited to Sean Hannity. In 1970, Cone published *A Black Theology of Liberation*. This book has been quite influential on Jeremiah Wright and the sermons he has delivered at Trinity United Church of Christ. In that book, Cone asserts the following:

> The definition of Jesus as black is crucial for christology if
> we truly believe in his continued presence today. Taking
> our clue from the historical Jesus who is pictured in the

New Testament as the Oppressed One, what else, except blackness, could adequately tell us the meaning of his presence today? Any statement about Jesus today that fails to consider blackness as the decisive factor about his person is a denial of the New Testament message. The life, death, and resurrection of Jesus reveal that he is the man for others, disclosing to them what is necessary for their liberation from oppression. If this is true, then Jesus Christ must be black so that blacks can know that their liberation is his liberation...

The black Christ is he who threatens the structure of evil as seen in white society, rebelling against it, thereby becoming the embodiment of what the black community knows that it must become...

To be a disciple of the black Christ is to become black with him. Looting, burning, or the destruction of white property are not primary concerns. Such matters can only be decided by the oppressed themselves who are seeking to develop their images of the black Christ...

Whites do not recognize what is happening, and they are thus unable to deal with it. For most whites in power, the black community is a nuisance –something to be considered only when the natives get restless. But what white America fails to realize is the explosive nature of the kingdom. Although its beginning is small, it will have far-reaching effects not only on the black community but on the white community as well. Now is the time to make decisions about loyalties, because soon it will be too late. Shall we or shall we not join the black revolutionary kingdom?[161]

In March 2008, the sermons of Dr. Jeremiah Wright began to be revealed by major media such as FOX News, ABC, and CNN. Videos of many of the sermons are proudly sold on Trinity United Church of Christ's website. Some of the sermons of Jeremiah Wright directly reflect the same sentiments echoed by James Cone. A year earlier, in March 2007, when he appeared on *Hannity & Colmes*, Jeremiah Wright indignantly asked Sean Hannity, "Do you know liberation theology? … Do you know black liberation theology? How many of Cone's books have you read?"

A year later, Wright's controversial comments about America, Hillary Clinton, and white America, preached from the pulpit, were broadcasted over the internet and eventually on all the major news stations. Much of the American media and many Americans began asking how much of this slander has influenced Barack Obama? However, very few of the major media has even questioned the ideology of liberation theology that is the foundation of this controversial church. Most of the American people, including most Christians, have not yet unearthed the fundamental tenets of this ideology and its influence on Senator Obama.

This all matters because this is the very church where Obama "got Christianity." All that Obama seems to know about Christianity has been informed by Trinity United Church of Christ in Chicago and its controversial pastor, Jeremiah Wright. How has this Marxist-inspired liberation theology influenced the Senator and his public policies?

## OBAMA'S "KINGDOM ON EARTH"

Part of Cardinal Ratzinger's major criticism of liberation theology was its insistence on the merging of politics with theology – particularly a radical politics of class warfare that seeks a total reinterpretation of the Christian reality. Marxism, the foundation of liberation theology, calls for a revolution that produces equality in the here and now and does not wait for God's kingdom or any other kind of afterlife. When you merge Marxism with Christianity you get liberation theology. When your entire worldview is guided by liberation theology, perhaps you get a statement like this: "I am confident we can create a Kingdom right here on earth."[162]

That statement about creating a "Kingdom right here on earth" was spoken by Barack Obama when talking about how he equates his faith with his public policies. It was part of the same speech given to the Redemption World Outreach Center in South Carolina, which was cited at the beginning of this chapter. The problem with that statement is that it is a Christian heresy.

Christianity has always held that in the Lord's Prayer (the "Our Father"), the statement, "Thy Kingdom come" has primarily referred to the final coming of the reign of God through Christ's return. In the New Testament, Jesus answered his disciples' questions about the Kingdom by saying: "My kingdom does not belong to this world. If my kingdom did belong to this world, my attendants (would) be fighting to keep me from being handed over to the Jews. But as it is, my kingdom is not here."

Jesus' testimony to us through the Gospel is clear. We should not be fighting for a Kingdom here on earth – as the liberation theologians would have us do. Jesus' "kingdom is not here." This does not mean we should not be striving to serve the poor or do the good works he asked us to do. Of course we should. But we do not need to violently overturn society or engage in class warfare to "create a Kingdom here on earth." Christians believe that we never shall find Utopia here – no matter how much some politicians, such as Obama, want us to.

***

The kind of Christianity Obama was attracted to at Trinity United Church of Christ – a liberation theology (and specifically, a black liberation theology) – is not in line with mainline Christianity. But, it is in line with Obama's far left political beliefs. This allows him to use the language of Christianity while still retaining the non-Christian belief of trying to create an egalitarian utopia here on earth.

In June 2008, Christian evangelical leader, James Dobson, accused Obama of distorting the Bible. "I think he's deliberately distorting the traditional understanding of the Bible to fit his own worldview, his own confused theology," Dobson said. "He is dragging biblical understanding through the gutter."[163]

The political ideology of liberation theology is a product of the left – it holds that we should use the government, or whatever force possible, to redistribute wealth and create a kingdom (or utopia) here on earth. Conveniently, this "theology" is in line with only one political ideology. More conveniently, because this ideology is implanted in a "church," it is viewed as "religious."

As Obama learned from his anthropologist mother, religion brings people together in community. From his own experience, he learned that the historically black church has been the center of the black community's political, economic, and spiritual life. Obama's political success in Chicago was built on his organizing around this powerful political force in the black community. His hope now is that his ability to capture the language of Christianity, a language which most American voters share on a national scale, will help him catapult into the White House and align their more proper view of Christianity with his political ideology.

## A RELIGIOUS DOUBLE STANDARD?

We began this chapter with Obama's statement that he does not believe the Democrat Party should "cede values and faith" to the Republican Party. Throughout his campaign, he has constantly used biblical language in his speeches, some of which come close to sounding like sermons. Yet, the media has not applied the same standard they typically apply to politicians on the right when they start talking religion.

Typically, the media portrays Christian politicians on the right, such as George W. Bush or Mike Huckabee, as anything from "intolerant" to "theocratic." But Obama gets away with his use of these religious references without the media questioning his religion or even his sincerity. Perhaps it is because he is okay with gay marriage, abortion, and an agenda which calls on government entitlement programs in the name of Christian charity. The kind of Christianity which Obama purports to believe is in line with his political prescriptions.

***

I have raised the importance of Obama's religious background – from his Muslim heritage to the liberation theology preached at Trinity United Church of Christ – because Obama uses so much biblical language in his speeches and texts. He has stated how much his church and his pastor have influenced him. (Remarkably, at the time this book was going to publication, Obama disassociated himself from his pastor and subsequently left his church, because of the political implications these associations were beginning to cause him). This church influenced Obama so much that he titled his book *The Audacity of Hope* after the title of a sermon delivered by his pastor Jeremiah Wright. Since he has self-claimed that his heritage and his faith experience have made him who he is, we as voters are obligated to question how it will influence his ideology, his character, and his public policies. Now, it is up to us to decide what to do about it.

146  Associated Press, "Election reinforces USA's religious schism," *USA Today*, http://www.usatoday.com/news/politicselections/2004-11-04-religion_x.htm, (4 November 2004).

147  Peter Hamby, "Obama: GOP doesn't own faith issue," *CNNPolitics.com*, http://www.cnn.com/2007/POLITICS/10/08/obama.faith, (8 October 2007).

148  Paul Watson, "Islam an unknown factor in Obama bid: Campaign downplays his connection during boyhood in Indonesia," *Los Angeles Times*, http://www.latimes.com/news/nationworld/nation/bal-te.oba ma16mar16,1,7181735,full.story?coll=la-headlines-nation, (16 March 2007).

149  Chris Welch, "Voter asks Obama about 'Muslim background'," *CNNPolitics.com*, http://politicalticker.blogs.cnn.com/2007/12/23/voter-asks-obama-about-muslim-background, (23 December 2007).

150  Barack Obama, *The Audacity of Hope* (New York: Crown Publishers, 2006), p. 204.

151  Ibid.

152  Ibid.

153  Obama, *The Audacity of Hope*, p. 273.

154  Obama, *The Audacity of Hope*, p. 204.

155  Paul Watson, "Islam an unknown factor in Obama bid: Campaign downplays his connection during boyhood in Indonesia," *Los Angeles Times*, http://www.latimes.com/news/nationworld/nation/bal-te.oba ma16mar16,1,7181735,full.story?coll=la-headlines-nation, (16 March 2007).

156  Obama, *The Audacity of Hope*, p. 206.

157  Obama, *The Audacity of Hope*, p. 207.

[158] Trinity United Church of Christ "About us" webpage, http://www.tucc. org/about.htm

[159] Jeremiah Wright, interview by Sean Hannity on *Hannity & Colmes* (Fox News Channel), http://www.foxnews.com/story/0,2933,256078,00. html
(2 March 2007).

[160] Cardinal Joseph Ratzinger, "Preliminary Notes on Liberation Theology," http://www.christendom-awake.org/pages/ratzinger/liberationtheol. htm, (Version: 9 December 2004).

[161] James Cone, *A Black Theology of Liberation* (Philadelphia: Lippincott, 1970).

[162] Peter Hamby, "Obama: GOP doesn't own faith issue," *CNNPolitics.com,* http://www.cnn.com/2007/POLITICS/10/08/obama.faith, (8 October 2007).

[163] Eric Gorski, "Dobson accuses Obama of 'distorting' Bible," *Associated Press My Way,* http://apnews.myway.com/article/20080624/ D91G8E200.html.

# CHAPTER 7

## BARACK OBAMA'S SOCIALIST POLICIES:
## HOW BELIEFS HAVE CONSEQUENCES

One's personal beliefs cannot be divorced from their public policies – even if that person intends them to be. This isn't to suggest that Obama (or any public figure) necessarily wants to use their public position to convert others to their beliefs (although that may be the case). But it is to suggest that one's worldview largely influences the decisions they make in office.

This particular chapter was chosen to follow the preceding one because it is intended to show how Obama's appeal to religious voters should make them wary – not only because he has been part of a fringe religious group for the past twenty years, but also because he and his church have conformed their religious beliefs to their preconceived political beliefs.

Obama isn't the first public official to try to appeal to religious sentiments to gain support for his public policies – and he certainly won't be the last. But, it is a very specific kind of religion at play here in Obama's beliefs. As demonstrated in the last chapter, Obama "got" Christianity in a very unusual place, by a very unusual pastor, who preached a very unusual theology. His is not the Christianity that is in line with mainstream Christianity. His is more in line with a Christian heresy that conforms not to God's will, but to man's.

In his speech on June 3, 2008, at the end of the primary season, Obama declared himself the presumptive nominee for the Democrat party. In that speech, he equated himself to a political messiah, when he said:

> I am absolutely certain that generations from now, we will be able to look back and tell our children that this was the moment when we began to provide care for the sick and good jobs to the jobless… This was the moment when the rise of the oceans began to slow and our planet began to heal; this was the moment when we ended a war and secured our nation and restored our image as the last, best hope on Earth.[164]

G.K. Chesterton once said, "When a Man stops believing in God, he doesn't then believe in nothing, he believes anything." For some on the left, the State has become their religion – where they put all their hopes; and Obama has become their messiah – the great savior that will "provide" care for the sick and jobs to the jobless, "slow" the rise of the oceans, and "heal" the planet. These are Obama's words. The almighty State, with Obama as its leader, will provide for us all, he and his followers proclaim.

Some religious voters may be tempted to vote for Obama because he speaks the Christian language to help the poor. But, remember, liberation theology (a Christian heresy) speaks much of the same language of doctrinal Christian theology, as it plays on the Christian call to serve the poor. However, liberation theology goes further – and so does Senator Obama.

The problem with Obama and many other politicians is they all play to the deep-seeded sentiments of Christian charity that we all admire. Their strategy: they make promises to us by listing what government programs they will enact to help the poor – sometimes this requires new programs, other times just more money for existing ones. They promise us that once they are placed at the paternal head of the government, they will begin dishing out these programs and we can all feel good that we are contributing and perhaps, partaking in them – because lately it seems that more than "the poor" want government to help them.

College students and young voters are most easily manipulated by smooth talking politicians who offer promises at no expense. It is no wonder that the Obama campaign, with its "change" message has seen many young voters follow them. College students are more easily swayed by politicians who want to reduce their educational and health care costs – through government subsidies. They don't realize, however, that someone (perhaps even them) will be picking up the tab through taxes and other fees. Instead of taking up the mantle of personal responsibility, some turn to government to be the provider. Of course we all want to help the needy and those who can't help themselves, but government programs stepped beyond that limited and specific responsibility a long time ago. An Obama presidency will only take government programs to a new level of entitlement.

In his speech on Super Tuesday, Senator Barack Obama told his audience "We are the change we seek."[165] Given his record and his prescriptions for change, Mr. Obama thinks more government is the solution. (This was discussed in detail in Steve Bierfeldt's chapter on government health care and Brendan Steinhauser's chapter on economic policy). In reality, the change Obama wants to deliver is good old-fashioned socialism. By redistributing wealth, Obama's policies build on the utopian idea that we can build a "kingdom here on earth." (This was referenced in my previous chapter on Obama's religion.)

I have a question for Mr. Obama: If "we" truly are "the change we seek" then why do "we" need government to enact that "change"? Wouldn't real change be relying on individual action? Wouldn't real change be reforming big government programs and helping "we the people" be *less* dependent on an already too large and too incompetent government? I would think Mr. Obama would agree. After all, in the same Super Tuesday speech he talked about the personal stories of how he and fellow community leaders in inner city Chicago got together to fix neighborhood problems. That didn't take government, it took individuals.

Hurricane Katrina is a prime example of how being dependent on government can lead to tragedy. The people of New Orleans, particularly the poor who lived in government housing projects and depended on welfare and other entitlement programs had always lived with the mindset of being dependent on government. Thus, when a hurricane hit, those same people thought the government would be there. It wasn't. Not on the local level, not on the state level, and not on the federal level. The New Orleans mindset of "depend on government" failed the people of New Orleans - particularly the poor. The government wasn't there for them. And, given the cycle of poverty that so many in this country live in, one has to ask: what exactly have big-government policies done to help the poor?

***

The idea in this chapter is plain and simple (and pretty obvious). Barack Obama's policies endorse the idea of big government solutions, social welfare, and the redistribution of income. Of course we all want better health care, better education, less poverty, and more prosperity. The question is: how do we go about it?

For Senator Obama, his solution is putting the leftist policies that align with the liberation theology preached at Trinity United Church into practice. He has already done so as an Illinois state senator and during his short time as a U.S. Senator; there is no reason to doubt that he'll continue these far left policies from the White House. For whatever reason, Obama sees injustice and believes he can solve it by using the power of government to take from those who have earned their wealth and give it to those who have not. As Senator Tom Coburn (R-OK) recently stated, "Spending other people's money is not compassionate."[166]

The true nature of Christian charity is the kind of charity that can be observed outside the sphere of government: in churches, neighborhood communities, and other intermediary associations. In *Democracy in America*, Alexis de Tocqueville observed that the greatest strength of America was not its government, but the voluntary associations that helped bring people together in strong communities. The more powerful government is, the less strong these voluntary associations are able to be; the stronger these voluntary associations are, the less need there is for government. The true nature of Christianity is then to work to lessen the power (and need) of government and strengthen our voluntary associations – the first step of which would be to promote, support and involve ourselves in them.

In Obama's own book, *The Audacity of Hope*, he claims he did this kind of community work with other leaders in the streets of Chicago. He continues to claim that what drew him to Trinity United Church was the good works the people from the church did for others in their community. If this is indeed true, then it is troubling that Obama would put his socialist ideology first over the non-government charity he actually experienced. What makes a bigger difference in rebuilding people's lives and ending the cycle of poverty: the church or the government? Charitable acts or government force?

Obama is on a messianic mission to "create a Kingdom here on earth." His track record demonstrates that he'll use government force if necessary. And that is exactly in line with the methods of those who put liberation theology into practice. It is precisely this reason that we must examine his questionable religion, his worldview, his far left voting record, and the people he surrounds himself with.

## Obama's Communist Mentor

In Obama's first book, *Dreams From My Father*, he writes about "a poet named Frank" who visited Obama and his family in Hawaii, read poetry and was full of "hard-earned knowledge" and advice. The only media outlet I could find that reported this was Accuracy in Media, a watchdog group that keeps the media in check. In his article, "Obama's Communist Mentor," Joe Cummings makes us aware that the "Frank" that Obama refers to is Frank Marshall Davis, a communist.[167]

Obama probably only gave us his first name, "Frank," so that people could not go and "Google" Frank Marshall Davis and discover that he was a communist. That might turn up some facts that aren't so popular with mainstream Americans. Davis was a known communist who belonged to a party subservient to the Soviet Union. The 1951 report of the Commission on Subversive Activities to the Legislature of the Territory of Hawaii identified Davis as a member of the Communist Party of the United States of America (CPUSA). The U.S. Congress' House Un-American Activities Committee accused Davis of involvement in several communist-front organizations. The documentation adds up, as Davis published pieces in CPUSA-supported publications and is on record defending communists.

Cummings also demonstrates that from the knowledge Obama had of Davis, he knew him well enough to know he was a communist and who he was associated with. Why? In *Dreams From My Father*, Obama describes "Frank" as someone who had "some modest notoriety once," and who was a "contemporary of Richard Wright and Langston Hughes during his years in Chicago..." (which is true of Davis). Obama goes further and says that "Frank and his old Black Power dashiki self" gave him advice before he left for Occidental College in 1979, at the age of 18.

What "advice" Davis gave Obama remains an open question. But, one noted left-wing professor who hangs out in communist circles, Gerarld Horne, articulated his understanding of the Davis-Obama relationship. Professor Horne is a contributing editor to the Communist party journal, *Political Affairs*.

In a speech he delivered in March 2007 at a CPUSA reception at NYU, Horne introduced the audience to Frank Marshall Davis and described his young mentor, the now-junior Senator from Illinois, Barack Obama:

> In any case, deploring these convictions in Hawaii was an African-American poet and journalist by the name of Frank Marshall Davis, who was certainly in the orbit of the CP – if not a member – and who was born in Kansas and spent a good deal of his adult life in Chicago, before decamping to Honolulu in 1948 at the suggestion of his good friend Paul Robeson. Eventually, he befriended another family – a Euro-American family – that had migrated to Honolulu

from Kansas and a young woman from this family
eventually had a child with a young student from Kenya
East Africa who goes by the name of Barack Obama,
who retracing the steps of Davis eventually decamped
to Chicago. In his best selling memoir 'Dreams of my
Father', the author speaks warmly of an older black poet,
he identifies simply as "Frank" as being a decisive influence
in helping him to find his present identity as an African-
American, a people who have been the least anticommunist
and the most left-leaning of any constituency in this nation
– though you would never know it from reading so-called
left journals of opinion. At some point in the future,
a teacher will add to her syllabus Barack's memoir and
instruct her students to read it alongside Frank Marshall
Davis' equally affecting memoir, "Living the Blues" and
when that day comes, I'm sure a future student will not
only examine critically the Frankenstein monsters that
US imperialism created in order to subdue Communist
parties but will also be moved to come to this historic and
wonderful archive in order to gain insight on what has
befallen this complex and intriguing planet on which we
reside.[168]

There is a load of material to unload here in Horne's speech. One must always keep things in context. That said, we must remember that Horne is almost giddy here, having so much hope that the communist agenda will be forwarded by a young man who was influenced by one of them. A young man who one day may be President and exert his influence on national policy.

Horne is so hopeful about this and so confident that Davis influenced Obama that he believes that "at some point in the future, a teacher will add" Davis' memoir *Living the Blues* to her syllabus to allow students to examine what ideas influenced the President of the United States. Horne is delivering the very point that this chapter opened up with: ideas have consequences. Many argue that the founding fathers of this nation were influenced by Greek philosophy, Roman law, the market economy of Italy, France, and England, and the idea of representation first presented in the Magna Carta. Horne believes Barack Obama was influenced by communism, the idea that the state should be the provider for the people. When we look at Obama's policies for "change," we might now be getting a better idea of what this "change" is going to look like.

Horne isn't alone. Left-wingers across this nation are celebrating the Obama candidacy. On a communist blog called "People's Weekly World," one post by Frank Chapman was excited about the "change" that may be coming to America. In response to Obama winning the Iowa caucus, he says, "Obama's victory was more than a progressive move; it was a dialectical leap in ushering in a qualitatively new era of struggle. Marx once compared revolutionary struggle with the work of the mole, who sometimes burrows so far beneath the ground that he leaves no trace of his movement on the surface. This is the old revolutionary 'mole,' not only showing his traces on the surface but also breaking through. The old pattern of politics as usual has been broken. It may not have happened as we expected it to happen but what matters is that it happened."[169]

## OBAMA'S INTERNATIONAL SOCIALIST CONNECTIONS

Socialists and communists are not just excited about Obama. The Senator from Illinois has a track record of working with them. According to Cliff Kincaid of Accuracy in Media, Obama "is in fact, an associate of a Chicago-based Marxist group with access to millions of labor union dollars and connections to expert political consultants, including a convicted swindler."[170] That group is the Chicago branch of the Democratic Socialists of America (DSA). They endorsed Obama in 1996, when he first ran for his a seat in the Illinois Senate. Just like the folks at Trinity United Church, the DSA has been with Obama since the beginning of his political career.

The Chicago DSA maintains close ties to two of its former members of the Students for a Democratic Society (SDS), Williams Ayers and Carl Davidson. The SDS is largely responsible for the radical leftist activism and anti-war protests on America's college campuses in the 1960s. The SDS spawned the Weather Underground organization, a domestic terrorist group which Ayers was a member. Ayers is now a college professor and served with Obama on the board of the Woods Fund of Chicago. Davidson is now on the Committees of Correspondence for Democracy and Socialism, an offshoot of the old Soviet-controlled CPUSA. Davidson helped organize the 2002 Chicago rally where Obama delivered a speech against the war in Iraq.

In February 2008, *The Politico* reported that Obama began his political campaign for the Illinois State Senate at a 1995 meeting at the home of William Ayers and his wife, Weather Underground sidekick Bernadine Dohrn. Obama was there because Ayers and Dohrn represented a few of the district's influential liberals.[171]

*The Washington Post* has reported that in April 2001, Ayers contributed $200 to Obama's re-election fund to the Illinois State Senate and that Ayers and Obama "lived within a few blocks of each other in the trendy Hyde Park section of Chicago, and moved in the same liberal-progressive circles."[172]

The Chicago DSA newsletter praised the fact that Obama, as a state senator, showed up to eulogize Saul Mendelson, a long-time socialist activist who was one of the "champions" of "Chiacago's democratic left." The DSA describes itself as "The largest socialist organization in the United States, and the principal US affiliate of the Socialist International." The Socialist International, according to its own website, "has consultative status with the United Nations, and works internationally with a large number of other organizations."

With this consultation, the United Nations frequently calls on the United States and other Western countries, to increase their aid to other countries. This connection is important because Obama introduced "The Global Poverty Act," which was rushed through the U.S. Senate's Foreign Relations Committee in February 2008, with the help of Senators Joe Biden, the chairman, and Republican Richard Lugar.[173] *Accuracy in Media* reports that this bill would commit the U.S. to spend more than $845 billion above and beyond what the U.S. already spends to help alleviate poverty abroad.[174] "The legislation would commit the U.S. to spending 0.7 percent of gross national product on foreign aid." They have dubbed it Barack Obama's "global tax proposal." (This was referenced in Brendan Steinhauser's chapter on Obama's foreign policy.) Perhaps this is a sign of executive decisions to come should Obama reach the White House.

***

Obama has learned from the best socialist activists available to him throughout his life. Early on, as he confesses, he received "advice" from a black communist, Frank Marshall Davis. Much like Obama, Davis lived in Kansas, Hawaii, and Chicago. Without a clear father figure of his own, Sigmund Freud might have us believe that Obama latched on to Davis, as a man who helped form the intellect of Obama as he emerged out of his youth and into academia.

As Obama moved into Chicago and became a "community organizer," he spent much time with prominent socialist groups and key socialist figures in Chicago's far left political circles. Once you put the pieces together, they all add up. With Barack Obama, we will not be getting someone who wants to simply rise above the right-left dichotomy to create a "new kind of politics," as he claims. Instead, we will be getting more of the same: a politician who has spent his life studying about and working for big government policies. Obama uses a lot of rhetoric about "change" and how we need to go in a different direction. The only direction he is going to take us on is towards an agenda that has not only been tried before, but one that has only proven a failure time and time again. It isn't change we can believe in.

# ENDNOTES

164  Campaign speech, St. Paul, MN, "Remarks of Senator Obama," http://www.barackobama.com/2008/06/03/remarks_of_senator_barack_obam_73.php, (3 June 2008).

165  CQ Transcripts Wire, "Obama on Super Tuesday: 'Our Time Has Come'," *Washington Post*, http://www.washingtonpost.com/wp-dyn/content/article/2008/02/06/AR2008020600199.html, (6 February 2008).

166  Tom Coburn, "Republicans Are in Denial," *Wall Street Journal*, http://online.wsj.com/article/SB121184690228421415.html?mod=rss_opinion_main, (27 May 2008), p A21.

167  Joe Cummings, "Obama's Communist Mentor," *Accuracy in Media*, http://www.aim.org/aim-column/obamas-communist-mentor, (18 February 2008).

168  Gerald Horne, "Rethinking the History and Future of the Communist Party," *Political Affairs*, http://www.politicalaffairs.net/article/articleview/5047/1/32/, (28 March 2007).

169  Joe Chapman, "After Iowa," *People's Weekly World*, Letters, http://www.pww.org/article/articleview/12302/1/405, (12 January 2008).

170  Cliff Kincaid, "Obama's International Socialist Connections," *Accuracy in Media*, http://www.aim.org/aim-column/obamas-international-socialist-connections, (14 February 2008).

171  Ben Smith, "Obama once visited '60s radicals," *The Politico*, http://www.politico.com/news/stories/0208/8630.html, (22 February 2008).

172  Michael Dobbs, "Obama's 'Weatherman 'Connection," *Washington Post*, The Fact Checker, http://blog.washingtonpost.com/fact-checker/2008/02/obamas_weatherman_connection.html, (19 February 2008).

173  United States Senate Bill 2433, (14 February 2008).

174  Cliff Kincaid, "Obama's Global Tax Proposal Up for Senate Vote," *Accuracy in Media*, http://www.aim.org/aim-column/obamas-global-tax-proposal-up-for-senate-vote/, (12 February 2008).

# CHAPTER 8

## MISPLACED LOYALTY:
## BARACK OBAMA'S LOST RECORDS

Barack Obama has repeatedly proclaimed a desire to bring transparency to Washington D.C. and the office of the President. Obama has declared himself as the candidate able to rise above partisan politics and unite our nation behind his leadership. With such a limited amount of political experience, however, Obama has been able to twist his statements and hide his far left voting record. By investigating Barack Obama further we find his promises of transparency are hollow. Obama is not a leader ready to direct this country for the next four years. Obama is merely a deceptive official, eager to further his political agenda by portraying himself as something other than what he really is. Talk of hope and change only goes as far as there is not a paper trail to expose one's intentions. It is that very paper trail from his time in the Illinois state Senate that Barack Obama has tried to eliminate.

In March of 2008 Barack Obama criticized his Democratic primary opponent Hillary Clinton for not releasing her tax records. In a letter to supporters Obama stated:

> Senator Clinton's refusal to release her taxes returns denies the media and the American people the opportunity to even begin that process. Though her campaign has tried to kick the issue down the road, Democratic voters deserve to know...[175]

Hillary Clinton released her tax records one month later, apparently satisfying Obama's desire for transparency in the race for the White House. However, questions soon arose concerning Barack Obama's own honesty on the campaign trail. In November of 2007 a political back and forth began concerning the files and documents Obama had kept during his time in the Illinois legislature. Elected in 1997, Obama spent eight years as an official from the prairie state's 13th district. With fewer than four years as a United States Senator his records as an Illinois official may provide Obama's critics with the best opportunity to expose his radical liberal agenda. Not surprisingly, it is those very records that Obama has tried to cover up.

At a press conference in Johnson, Iowa in November of 2007, Lynn Sweet of the *Chicago Sun Times* questioned Barack Obama. Sweet inquired of Obama's personal documents from the Illinois state Senate and where they could currently be found. While this would seem like a simple request of a candidate that has campaigned on a message of changing Washington and bringing back transparency to the political scene, what would follow would be the first in a long string of half-truths and deceptive responses by Obama and his campaign staff. Obama replied he had only one staff member assigned during his tenure and did not have sufficient resources to keep that information. He stated, "I don't have the Barack Obama state Senate library available to me. I do not have a whole bunch of records from those years."[176]

Sweet pressed the matter further, asking not for specifics but only where the records might be located. Unwilling to yield, Obama replied, "You know I'm not certain Lynn. I didn't have the resources to ensure all this stuff was archived in some way; it could have been thrown out. I haven't been in the state Senate for some time. I'm not sure Lynn, I don't know."[177] Taylor Pensoneau, a historian who has written about Illinois legislators and governors, questions Obama's excuses. "Most of those guys do keep this stuff, especially the favorable stuff. They've all got egos," he said. "It goes in scrapbooks or maybe boxes. I don't think it's normal practice to say it's all discarded."[178] In contrast, Hillary Clinton and husband Bill have an estimated file at the National Archives of 78 million pages of documents and 20 million email messages.[179]

Perhaps even more interesting than Obama's claim of ignorance was its conflict with a previous statement made by his own staff. Earlier in 2007, campaign spokesman Ben LaBolt asked *The Associated Press* to narrow a request for records on whether Obama had ever urged clemency for a convicted criminal. "You're asking us to do an extremely exhaustive search into every record we have from the U.S. Senate and state Senate offices," LaBolt said at the time.[180] Sensing an opening for the media and opponents to latch onto, the Obama campaign quickly shifted into damage control mode.

On the November 11, 2007 edition of *Meet the Press,* host Tim Russert continued with the line of questioning Sweet had done two days prior. When asked where his records were, Obama again stated they were not kept. Pressed by Russert, Obama said, "Well let's be clear, in the state Senate, every single piece of information, every document related to state government was kept by the state of Illinois and has been disclosed and is available and has been gone through with a fine-toothed comb by news outlets in Illinois. The stuff that I did not keep has to do with, for example, my schedule..." [181] Russert continued to push for more of the story, asking "But your meetings with lobbyists and so forth, there's no record of that?" Obama replied, "I did not have a scheduler, but, as I said, every document related to my interactions with government is available now."[182]

Seeing the hole in their argument beginning to widen, that evening the Obama camp had changed their story yet again, claiming the records were indeed kept by the state of Illinois and passed on to Obama's next in line in the legislature. Only a few hours after Obama's appearance on *Meet the Press,* senior strategist David Axelrod claimed, "files pertinent to ongoing casework were passed to Kwame Raoul, his successor."[183]

With the political double talk becoming a tidal wave, some news outlets descended upon the story of Obama's "lost records," with the educational foundation Judicial Watch taking on the case in February of 2008. Though admittedly referring to itself as a conservative organization, Judicial Watch's focus is to promote, "transparency, accountability, and integrity in government, politics, and the law."[184] Judicial Watch has gone after Republicans and Democrats alike, even suing to require the Bush administration to release its energy task force documents in 2002.[185] On February 7, 2008 Judicial Watch filed a Freedom of Information Act request with the Illinois State Archives. In the letter, Judicial Watch asked for:

> Any and all public documents, as defined by 5 ILCS
> 140/2c, resulting from Illinois state Senator Barack
> Obama's years in the office (1997-2004) that the ISA have
> in their possession.[186]

The response came on Feb 25, 2008 via Donna Leonard, Executive Council to the Illinois Secretary of State Jesse White. In the letter Ms. Leonard stated that contrary to the claims of the Obama camp, the state of Illinois had no such records. She wrote:

> Please be advised that the ISA maintains the official records
> of the Illinois General Assembly. These records are not
> specific to Senator Obama. The ISA does not maintain
> Senator Obama's personal records or papers nor does the
> ISA maintain records generated by his office. In addition,
> the ISA has received no requests from Senator Obama to
> archive any records formerly in his possession. If there are
> specific records you seek, lease amend your request and
> include the names of the individual documents you seek.[187]

Unwilling to accept this answer, Judicial Watch expanded their investigation, delivering a letter to the office of Obama's successor in the Illinois state Senate, Kwame Raoul. The letter requested the records Obama's strategist David Axelrod had claimed Mr. Raoul was keeping. Judicial Watch asked for:

> All records and/or files from former State senator Barack
> Obama to state Senator Kwame Raoul upon succeeding
> Mr. Obama in 2004.

On March 5th, 2008 Judicial Watch received a response from the state Senator of Illinois' 13th district. Despite Obama's assertions, Raoul did not have any such records either. He wrote:

> I am not currently in possession of any of the records and/or files that you are seeking. Any documents that I would have inherited from Senator Obama, would have been constituent work files, and those were reviewed and discarded upon me taking office.

Kwame Raoul further explained that even *if* he had such documents, he was under no legal obligation to turn them over. As an individual Senator, Mr. Raoul claimed he was not subject to the Freedom of Information Act with the Act only applying to "public bodies" and not legislators. He continued:

> Assuming arguendo that I was in possession of such materials, the materials are 'not public records' as defined under the Act, and are therefore not subject to disclosure...[188]

Tom Fitton, President of Judicial Watch believes Obama has a serious problem being forthcoming with his records. Fitton stated, "Our investigation suggests Senator Obama could have had his records archived so that they are available to the public, but, to this day, has chosen not to do so. Apparently, he does not want a complete paper trail of his time in the Illinois State Senate. Where are his office records?"[189]

Despite criticizing others for not making their records public, Barack Obama has attempted to hide his own files while serving as a state Senator. His hypocrisy and dishonesty are far reaching and do not adhere to the openness Obama has guaranteed. Promises must never be allowed to act as a substitute for real leadership. Obama has portrayed himself as the candidate who will unite the nation, but instead is nothing more than a man in the same model as countless bureaucrats who have come before him. With fewer than four years as a U.S. Senator and a record in the Illinois legislature that he has constantly tried to hide, Barack Obama is not the symbol of hope for our nation. He cannot be trusted to hold this country's highest office and serve as the most powerful man in the world.

[175] "Obama Campaign Goes After Clinton's Tax Records," Election Geek, http://www.electiongeek.com/blog/2008/03/05/obama-campaign-goes-after-clintons-tax-records/, (5 March 2008).

[176] Aswini Anburajan, "Obama on his State Senate Records," MSNBC First Read, http://firstread.msnbc.msn.com/archive/2007/11/09/457959.aspx (9 November 2007).

[177] Ibid.

[178] "Obama says he has no records from Ill. State Senate," First Amendment Center, http://www.firstamendmentcenter.org/news.aspx?id=19331 (16 November 2007).

[179] Ibid.

[180] Ibid.

[181] "Meet the Press transcript for Nov. 11, 2008," Meet the Press, http://www.msnbc.msn.com/id/21738432/ (11 November 2007).

[182] Ibid.

[183] Mike Allen, "Obama records requests prove fruitless," Politico, http://www.suntimes.com/news/sweet/645635,CST-NWS-sweet12.article (11 November 2007).

[184] "About Us," Judicial Watch, http://www.judicialwatch.org/about.shtml.

[185] http://news.bbc.co.uk/2/hi/americas/2119129.stm.

[186] "Anti-corruption group sues Cheney," BBC News, http://www.judicialwatch.org/files/2007/03%2008Illinois%20State%20Senator%20Obama.pdf (10 July 2002).

[187] "Re: Freedom of Information Act Request," Office of the Secretary of State, http://www.judicialwatch.org/files/2007/03%2008Illinois%20State%20Senator%20Obama.pdf (25 February 2008).

[188] "Re: Freedom of Information Act Request (February 20, 2008)" Kwame Raoul State Senator 13th District http://www.judicialwatch.org/files/2007/03%2008Raoul_ObamaRecordsResp1_0.pdf (5 March 2008).

[189] "Illinois State Archives Letter Raises Questions about Obama's Records Claim," Judicial Watch, http://www.judicialwatch.org/illinois-state-archives-letter-raises-questions-about-obama-s-records-claim (27 March 2008).

# Conclusion

## The Keys to the White House
## Are In Your Hands

"… Of those men who have overturned the liberties of
republics the greatest number have begun their career, by
paying an obsequious court to the people; commencing
Demagogues, and ending Tyrants."

- Alexander Hamilton, *Federalist #1*

More than 220 years ago, a group of colonial leaders gathered in Philadelphia
to construct a constitution for our young nation as it recently emerged out of
a war of independence from Great Britain. Historians concur that these men
exuded greatness. They were not only courageous to stand as rebels against
an imperial government that gave them no representation in Parliament,
but they were also men of great intellect. As Alexander Hamilton's quote
above reflects, these were men who were not only making history, but were
well aware of history.

Our rising generation today is fortunate enough to stand on the shoulders
of the many generations before us that built America. Of course, that "first
generation" of founders was made up of such unique men, who were so
intellectually equipped to put together perhaps the greatest document made
by men, the U.S. Constitution. Our Constitution has endured the test of
many tumultuous times. It now faces even graver threats from a government
that is beginning to be ruled by men, not by laws, reversing the standard set

by men like John Adams. Today, it has become commonplace for just five Supreme Court justices to overturn legislation and create new laws.

Perhaps the most unique element of the U.S. Constitution is the separation of powers. The branches of government were separated and each endowed with their own specific functions for particular reasons. If you need any proof, we urge you to consult *The Federalist Papers*, written by Hamilton, James Madison, and John Jay. These papers were created to make an argument to support the new federal constitution at a time when the young nation was only bounded by a very loose construction ordered by the weak Articles of Confederation. But these papers – all 85 of them – go further, and outline the expressed purpose of every article in the U.S. Constitution.

Since our founding, great Americans have risen in every generation, to serve in various offices and on many battlefields across the globe, to protect the vision that our founders had; the vision of what good government looks like; the vision that created the ideal free society. Our founders wanted us to pass on the office of the Presidency to men who best represented us as a people. As Hamilton put it in *Federalist 69*, "The process of election affords a moral certainty, that the office of the president will seldom fall to the lot of any man who is not in an eminent degree endowed with the requisite qualifications." While Hamilton was referring to the importance of the electoral process, including the system of the Electoral College in electing such a man, we can see the esteem that our founders had for the highest office in the land and the kind of people they wished to see fill that office (their ideal was George Washington). They wanted men of principle, men who could be trusted, men who would be knowledgeable and appreciative of the history of our institutions, and men who had the proper qualifications.

After examining the facts that we have presented in this book, it is hard to believe that the founders would have wanted to see us hand over the sacred keys of the White House to an inexperienced, ambitious demagogue such as Barack Obama. He is a man that we, as a country, have not yet had the chance to get to know well enough. He would certainly be one of the youngest Presidents, but his youth is not the only reason he is inexperienced. He has not yet been fully tested to make the decisions that are required of a Commander-in-Chief. And, just as importantly, perhaps more so, he has not yet been fully vetted.

We have tried to do our part in this book, given the demands on our time and resources, to put together the facts available and let you, the reader, have the ability to ponder such facts. We found it very difficult to gather these facts, as there were few media outlets that have reported such findings. We realized that right-wing talk show hosts and left-wing academics and media would each have their own talking points either for or against Obama simply based on his Democrat party label. But, Obama has talked a lot about the need for our country to try to rise above the typical left and right, and we accepted his challenge to do so. What we have found is that he has not done this himself. He talks a good game, but he plays quite another one.

We presented you with elements from his voting record during his time as an Illinois State Senator and during his few short years in the U.S. Senate. If you think we have presented any falsehoods or made any misrepresentations, we challenge you to hold us accountable. However, we are confident in our research and our sources, and in our ability to make the case against Obama based on the stubborn facts.

Speaking of facts: while Obama quite often talks about his time in the Illinois State Senate and the need to have an open, transparent government, he has done quite a lot to try to hide his own political and private records. He hasn't even reached the White House yet, and he is already trying to hide records. What will he do from the most powerful position in the free world?

Due to his short political career and his lack of experience, much of our book has relied on Obama's own words, from his published books, speeches, and interviews. After all, it was Obama who proclaimed "Don't tell me words don't matter." We could have certainly provided you with the words of those most closely associated with him, such as his controversial preacher Jeremiah Wright, or his outspoken wife and potential First Lady, Michelle Obama. But, we wanted to keep this focused on the junior Senator from Illinois. We do, however, believe, as our parents once preached to us, that you can learn much about a person by who they are associated with. The questionable friends that Obama has kept over the years should raise some serious alarms. They include controversial preachers like Jeremiah Wright and Father Michael Phleger, domestic terrorists such as William Ayers and Bernadine Dohrn of the Weather Underground, and shady businessmen like Tony Rezko and James Johnson.

We simply know too little about this man, and based on what we do know about him – his background, his questionable associations, and his far left voting record – we are not willing to entrust such a man with the sacred keys to the White House. The American Presidency comes with an awesome power and responsibility. As our founders intended, this office should only be given to someone who best represents us, someone we trust, and someone with high character. Obama's voting record is far to the left and way outside of the mainstream. He has shown a complete disdain for average Americans living in small towns and a complete disrespect for human life at its most fragile periods of birth and childhood development. He would overturn 220 years of sacrifice for a Constitution made of laws, not of men.

Our generation cannot let such a man be President. If "change" is what we seek, then it must be change within a tradition, a tradition of ordered liberty. We have strayed so far from our founders' intentions, that it is time that we stand up for change and ask that our individual liberties be granted once again. It is time for a new revolution indeed: a revolution that gets us back to the proper role of government.

At the high point of their grievances, our founders did not originally seek to be separated from England. They simply sought to confirm their rights as Englishmen. The revolution they started began as a return to the tradition of self-government, the proper role of government, and their proper places in that free society. They were seeking change, not for the sake of change, but for the sake of returning to the tradition of a people ruled by laws, not by men. For this purpose, we write this book, to prevent men of ambition from usurping more of our rights, our property, and our liberties from us. We hope you too, will join our cause. The keys to the White House are in your hands.

# Author Biographies

**Steve Bierfeldt** graduated Magna Cum Laude from Sacred Heart University in Fairfield, Connecticut in 2006. Soon afterward he moved to Arlington, Virginia and began work as National Field Director for the Leadership Institute, an organization with the expressed mission to "Identify, recruit, train and place conservative in politics, government and the media."

Under Steve's direction, the Leadership Institute's Field Program aided more than 1,000 conservative college organizations in all 50 states and provided more than 4.5 million college students with access to a conservative organization on their campus.

In March 2008 Steve was asked to manage the campaign for Amit Singh, a Republican candidate for US Congress in Virginia's 8th District. The campaign focused on the principles of limited government, fiscal responsibility, strong national defense and personal freedoms.

Steve has spoken at dozens of campuses throughout the country and has trained students at a number of seminars and conventions. Some of these include California Students for Life's "Celebrate Life Conference," the Conservative Political Action Conference in Washington DC, (CPAC) and numerous Leadership Institute "Student Activism Conferences."

Steve is currently working for Young Americans for Liberty, an intricate part of the newly formed Campaign for Liberty that has emerged from the Ron Paul 2008 Presidential Campaign. Young Americans for Liberty strives to educate and empower youth activists to promote the God-given rights of life, liberty, and property as set forth in the United States Constitution. Steve currently resides in Arlington, Virginia.

**Francisco Gonzalez** is the Director of Development for The James Madison Institute, Florida's premier free-market think-tank, based in Tallahassee, FL. A native Floridian, Francisco graduated cum laude from Florida Atlantic University with a bachelor's degree in History. Francisco earned an M.A. in History from the University of Maryland, where he also founded and was managing editor of *The Terrapin Times*, an award-winning conservative student newspaper.

From 2004-2007, Francisco was Director of Membership and Campus Leadership for the Intercollegiate Studies Institute in Wilmington, Delaware. At ISI, Francisco traveled to more than 30 states, helping conservative students and faculty members on hundreds of college campuses to start and organize groups focused on promoting our nation's founding principles. These groups ranged from free-market economics reading clubs, to active conservative campus groups, to forums that hosted speakers committed to furthering the principles of individual liberty and limited government and intellectually battling against the dangerous ideologies of collectivism and moral relativism. In 2007, Francisco joined ISI's development team, working to gain support for ISI's mission "to educate for liberty" on college campuses.

Through his work in the conservative movement, Francisco has appeared on MSNBC and C-SPAN, and has twice spoken at the Conservative Political Action Conference, the largest annual gathering of conservatives in Washington, D.C. His articles have also been published at conservativebattleline.com, centerforajustsociety.org, campusmagazine. org, and numerous other outlets. In June 2007, Francisco "filled in" for Presidential candidate, Senator Sam Brownback (R-KS), speaking on behalf of the Senator at the annual New Hampshire Republican Party dinner in Manchester. In January 2008, Francisco moved back to his beloved home state of Florida to join The James Madison Institute. He currently resides in Tallahassee, Florida.

**Brendan Steinhauser** is the Director of Federal and State Campaigns for FreedomWorks. He graduated Phi Beta Kappa from The University of Texas, where he led the UT chapter of The Young Conservatives of Texas. Brendan received university honors and was inducted into the National Society for Collegiate Scholars and the Golden Key International Honour Society.

While at UT, Brendan studied International Relations and American and European History. He was a staff writer for two Collegiate Network journals: *The Austin Review* and *Contumacy*. He founded Students for American Values and co-founded Students for a Colorblind America at UT, and was subsequently awarded the Free Republic Collegiate Eagle Award. Brendan worked as a reporter for GalleryWatch.com and spent one summer as an intern in the Texas House of Representatives.

Upon graduation, Brendan published his book *The Conservative Revolution: How to Win the Battle for College Campuses.* The book is a guide for student leaders who want to organize conservative clubs on their own campuses. The book's ideas for recruitment, events and public relations have impacted students on hundreds of college campuses across the country.

Brendan is an alumnus of both the Intercollegiate Studies Institute and the Leadership Institute. He was a co-founder of the ISI Young Alumni Association in Washington, D.C. and is a frequent guest lecturer at the LI Youth Leadership Schools. Brendan continues to advise student groups throughout the country, including chapters of The Young Conservatives of Texas, Students for Saving Social Security, College Republicans and Protest Warrior.

Brendan's articles on various topics have appeared in *Human Events*, TownHall.com, *Enter Stage Right*, *Front Page Magazine*, *The Daily Texan*, *The San Antonio Review*, Intellectual Conservative.com, FreedomWorks. org, CommonConservative.com, *The Houston Review*, GOPUSA.com and *Exotic Wildlife Magazine*. His personal website is TheConservativ eRevolution.com. Brendan resides in Alexandria, Virginia but says his heart remains in Texas.

# Acknowledgements

We would like to encourage readers of this book to always choose principles over party loyalty or political desire.

We would like to acknowledge the efforts of Ms. Mary Ellen Burke in providing copy editing assistance for the chapters by Steve Bierfeldt; and to Ryan Sorba for his research that contributed to the chapter on the family by Francisco Gonzalez.

We would also like to thank the thousands of young voters who inspired us to write this book; and our nation's founders who sacrificed everything so that we would have the opportunities to express ourselves freely and independently and participate in the great experiment of self-government.

Of course, family comes first and we would like to above all thank all of our family members for their love and encouragement. And nothing would be possible without Jesus Christ, the Lord, to whom we are forever grateful for the blessings and opportunities He has bestowed on us.

Printed in the United States
123670LV00012B/343-351/P